250 Ways To Be Romantic

250 Ways To Be Romantic

ISBN# 0-9625593-0-X

Made in USA

B. R. Publishing Co.
Century Village
Newport Q Suite 1077
Deerfield Beach, FL 33442

Special Appreciation to:
Kim Morris Lain
Susan Lawson
Steve Harvey
Mickey Wesserman
Julia Williamson
Lisa Barlet
Wally and Irene Anderson
Brian Gillus

Pictured on Cover:
Beth Ely
Scott Turner

Edited by:
Mark Hatmaker

TABLE OF CONTENTS

Introduction
Chapter 1
Birthdays, Anniversaries, and Proposals

Chapter Two
Gifts and Props

Chapter Three
Making Up

Chapter Four
Advertising

Chapter Five
Trips

Chapter Six
Food

Chapter Seven
An Assortment of Ideas on Romance

Chapter Eight

Introduction

Romance is indeed the spice of life! Without romance, life would be rather dull, uneventful, or, I guess you could say just down-right boring. On that we can all agree. But wait a minute! If everyone was a romantic, I suppose romancing the one you love wouldn't be all it's cranked up to be, because everyone would be so accustomed to it.

The thing is, everyone is not a romantic and those who are unique individuals and will never be commonplace. Those of you that are romantics are lucky indeed, and those who have a true romantic for a lover are luckier still!

People who aren't romantics wish they could be, and what they fail to realize is they can be with only a little effort and imagination. Male or female, it makes no difference. We all have an innate ability to be a romantic. In so many cases that capability is held in abeyance by us, so it lies dormant, existing inside, but seldom exercised. I say it's time for a revival of the state of romance and the main purpose of this book is to help you closet romantics to come out and declare yourselves, and to help with a few imaginative ideas intended to put you on a roll. Once you're on that roll, you can add some of your own concepts, thoughts, and inspirations to really fulfill the life of your lover.

Webster's New Collegiate Dictionary defines romance as an emotional attraction or aura belonging to an adventure or calling. It further states that "romance" means to exaggerate or invent detail or incident.

It defines a romantic as: VISIONARY, marked by the imaginative or emotional appeal of the heroic, adventurous, remote, mysterious, or idealized.

I would like to point out that the first step to romance is of course love. A list of synonyms for love could run on and on; here are some examples: affection, passion, tenderness, attachment, emotion, charity, sentiment, gratification, fondness, devotion, warmth, infatuation, ardor, yearning, joy, attraction, delight, worship, regard, fervor, adoration, and above all, friendship.

Romance is a state of mind and all it takes is some exaggeration in events or details to capture the heart and mind of your lover. The above list of love synonyms are key words for the romantic.

Each romantic notion we have can only be incited into action or accelerated to growth by one of these words.

Love, by simplest definition, is to care more for the feelings and well being of the other than you do for your own.

With this in mind, the true romantic is sentimental, chimerical, imaginative, fanciful, idealistic, poetic, artistic, and even extravagant and fictional when need be.

He/She is these things because of the spirit and nature that these words inspire within him/her to make certain the feelings and well being of his/her mate is complete, satisfied, not left wanting. In other words, a romantic is someone in love.

For those of you who feel a strain in your relationship and an ever widening gap in the ties that bind the hearts of love, retrieving your lover and putting the relationship back to the point it was when the two of you truly worshiped each other only takes a little romance.

For those who feel secure in their relationship, a little romance will only enhance that feeling of security.

So sit back, read, digest, enjoy, then take Barry's romantic ideas, couple them with your own romantic notions, and act. The end result will be that both you and your lover will be ever thankful that you did.

—A. Wayne Potter

CHAPTER ONE
BIRTHDAYS, ANNIVERSARIES, AND PROPOSALS

The ultimate destination of most affairs of the heart, the ones where true love prevails, is the altar. When the affair has reached the point where marriage is the next logical step, there has to be a proposal of marriage. The more romantic the proposal, the better the chances of your receiving the answer of "YES" that you're looking for and hope to acquire. This chapter deals with romantic ways to propose marriage with the hopes that you can take these ideas, add your own personal touch, capture the heart and soul of your lover, and live happily-ever-after. This chapter also gives ideas on how to make birthdays, anniversaries, and other holidays unforgettable romantic moments in the life of your lover.

♡1 Burned with Love

If you have found the love of your life and want to propose marriage, but for some reason, the right words just won't come out, get burned with love!

The way you handle that is to have a friend tape the words "Will you marry me?" to your back with white first-aid tape, the type you can find at the local drug-store. After the tape is applied, lie out in the sun with your back exposed to the rays.

Once you have sufficiently burned to the point where the words do show, you're home free. That evening, have a romantic dinner planned, and in your dinner conversation get around to the point that your back is burning. After dinner, ask your love interest if she will rub your back down with some soothing lotion.

Once the top is raised and the white skinned letters flash the message from the reddened background as though it were highlighted in neon, you have captured the heart and soul of your lover. Nothing but an affirmative answer will come! No one in love could ever turn down such a romantic proposal!

♡2 A Brass Band Proposal

Get a pick-up truck to haul them in, then hire a brass band to play the background music for your marriage proposal.

Make a large banner that says, "WILL YOU MARRY ME?" and hang it over the length of the truck (from front bumper to rear).

Rent a tuxedo to wear, then pull up in front of your lover's house or in front of her place of work just as she is getting off in the afternoon. The brass band will be playing even before you arrive on the scene and will of course continue to play as you pull up. Get down on one knee, reach out and hold the hand of your lover, and with the band playing a suitable tune for the occasion, ask for her hand in marriage.

Don't forget to have the engagement ring in the inside coat pocket of the tuxedo, and when your lover accepts your proposal, place the ring on her finger.

It will be a proposal she will never forget!

③ Window Proposal

In many old movies in which there was a marriage proposal involved in the script, it was made from a ladder at the bride-to-be's bedroom window.

The groom-to-be would take a few small pebbles, toss them gently against the window, (to wake his lover) climb the ladder, and pop the big question.

We've all seen it in the movies. It's an old-fashioned way of proposing but just as romantic today as ever.

If your lover's bedroom is on the second story of her house or apartment complex, copy the star of the old movie scripts and climb that ladder for your leading lady. If she sleeps on the ground floor, no problem; you can still toss the pebbles or knock gently at the window to ask for her hand in marriage.

To add a slice of romance to the already romantic idea, you may choose to:

(A) Pick out a suitable song befitting the occasion and sing it to her from just outside the window, then pop the big question.

(B) Write your own love song and sing it to her before asking for her hand in marriage.

(C) Strum the guitar as you sing your song. If you don't play, hire someone to play along as you sing or hire a violinist to play in the background.

(D) Carry a lantern with you to add a little romantic lighting.

(E) If your lover is on the ground floor and you don't have to use the ladder, don't forget to get down on one knee when asking the big question.

On the night of your proposal, there are two items you must never forget! One, a dozen roses to present your lover, and two, the engagement ring to place on her finger once she accepts your invitation to marry you.

You can use this idea even if you're living with your lover by saying you'll be home late that evening (for whatever reason) and for her not to wait up for you. Then when she's in bed, go to work.

This idea is also good for a married couple because the husband can use it to ask his wife to go away with him on a second honeymoon, or to ask, "Will you marry me again?" It's romantic and she's sure to love the idea.

④ An Old-fashioned Marriage Proposal

An old-fashioned way to propose marriage, but a way that is forever romantic and seems to never go out of style, is to take your lover to dinner, order a bottle of champagne, and have it arranged with the waiter to have the engagement ring in the bottom of your lover's glass.

Propose a toast to the two of you. When your lover turns up the glass and sees the ring, you ask her for her hand in marriage.

4

⑤ The Horse Drawn Proposal

A very imaginative way to propose marriage is to take a horse and buggy tour. Many cities have these. They are very popular in New York City, and they take you on a tour of Central Park.

If your city doesn't have this service, there is sure to be a nearby city that does, so you can take your lover on a short trip to one of those places.

Once you have reached your destination, tell the driver of the buggy what you have in mind. As he takes you on the tour, he will announce what each stop on the tour is and what historical value each place has.

You can take a tape player and champagne along, play some soft romantic music as you enjoy the ride, and at the right time, the driver will stop in front of some house and announce, "In this very spot, on this very date, Mr. (your name) asked Miss (your lover's name) for her hand in marriage."

At that time, you take out the engagement ring and ask your lover to marry you. Then, take out the champagne and celebrate the occasion.

It's a romantic way of doing it and no one could turn down such a romantic marriage proposal.

⑥ Pass the Message

A unique way to pass a message to your lover is to buy some nice napkins, then take them to a printer and have them print the message you want to give on them.

Once you've done this, make reservations at a nice restaurant, but before you and your lover go out to dinner, stop by the establishment, tell the manager what you have in mind, and give them a few of the special napkins to place in front of your lover when they seat you.

The personal message can be anything you'd like to say to your lover, from a simple "I love you", to a "Happy Birthday", or "Happy Anniversary."

This idea is also a great way to propose marriage by having "Will you marry me?" printed on the napkins.

You can use the special napkins at a dinner at home, or on a picnic if you would prefer that to making dinner reservations.

Whichever you decide is best for you and your lover, they will love the way you passed the message.

⑦ Pizza Proposal

Call up one of the local pizza delivery services and set this idea up with them in advance.

Once they agree to it, take them a white left hand glove and the engagement ring you have purchased for your lover for them to place in the pizza box, which they will later deliver.

Make arrangements with them to prepare a pizza with the words "Will you marry me?" spelled out on top with your lover's favorite topping, place the engagement ring on the ring finger of the glove, place the glove on top of the pizza, and deliver it later that evening (when you call).

Once you and your lover have settled in and are ready to eat, call in your order. Once delivered, give your lover the money to pay and tip the delivery person (so they will be the one to open the box) and look at the surprise on her face when she sees what you've been up to, and just what you have in mind.

You can also use this idea to just say "I love you", by having the pizza place spell it out with topping and deliver it to your lover.

⑧ Stained-Glass Proposal

Go to a store that specializes in making stained-glass designs and signs and have them make one that says, "Will you marry me?" Have it gift wrapped and present it to your lover at an opportune time. It's a unique way to propose to your lover if you can't muster up the nerve to just come out and ask.

You can also use this idea to just say, "I love you" by having those words put on the stained-glass.

Whatever you have written on the stained-glass, it will make a beautiful keepsake that your lover can hang on the wall to cherish forever.

♡9 A Neon Proposal

To light up a special message to your lover, go to an establishment which makes neon signs and have them make a neon light that conveys that special message you want.

It can just say, "I love you!" Or you can use it to ask for their hand in marriage by having one made that says, "Will you marry me?"

After you have your neon message made, you can hang it on the wall above your lover's bed, plug it in, and shut the bedroom door. When they walk in that afternoon after getting off from work, there it is. Your message in neon. They can't miss it.

You may choose to put the neon sign on the front of the house or apartment in which they live so it will be seen as soon as they drive up; or, if you own a boat, you can have the sign on the boat and ask your lover to go for a ride. When they see the sign, (no matter which place you chose to place it) they'll love it.

♡10 A Flashing Proposal

To propose marriage to your lover in flashing lights, take some pieces of quarter-inch styrofoam and cut the letters out to spell "WILL YOU MARRY ME?" Use styrofoam large enough so that each letter can be seen from about thirty yards away.

Once you have the letters cut out, put Christmas lights around the edge of each letter by pushing the lights through the styrofoam from the back side. This way, the cords are hidden and only the lights show on the front of your letters.

Run an extension cord to the front yard of your lovers house or to the parking lot of her apartment complex. Plug the cord into a flasher so the lighted message will flash on and off.

When your lover drives up as she comes home from work,

there will be "WILL YOU MARRY ME?" all lit up for her.

There are some options to this idea. You don't have to use the flasher if you would prefer the message to stay lit instead of flashing on and off. You can attach the letters to the side of the house or apartment by hanging the cords of the Christmas lights on small tacks placed on the side of the building instead of standing the letters in the yard with small stakes.

Also, if you would like your flashing proposal to be more private, you can hang the letters inside the house (such as over the bed, etc.).

Which way you decide to do it doesn't really matter; she'll get the message.

(11) A Floating Proposal

Most florists, and many department stores have silver helium filled balloons with messages printed on them. You can use these as a romantic way to propose marriage by buying several of the ones which say "I love you" on them, then, one which says "Will you marry me?"

Cut several pieces of red ribbon at lengths of about two feet each and tie the ribbon to the ends of the balloons that say "I love you." Cut one piece of ribbon three feet long and tie it to the end of the balloon which says "Will you marry me?"

Once you have done this, curl the lengths of ribbon, tie them all together, and you have a bouquet of balloons with all the "I love you" and one which says "Will you marry me?" rising above the others.

Gift wrap the ring box which contains the engagement ring, tie a piece of ribbon around the box, and tie it to the balloon bouquet so it hangs from the bottom.

Have the bouquet delivered to your lover and once you know she has received your floating proposal, call her up, say

9

how much you love her, and get the answer to your proposal.

These balloons come in different sizes, and to celebrate an anniversary or birthday, you may prefer the small balloons to the larger ones.

With the smaller balloons, you still make the bouquet the same way, with all the "I love you" balloons on ribbons of the same lengths; then put a balloon that says "Happy anniversary" or "Happy birthday" on the longer length of ribbon so it rises above the others. Then attach the gift to the bottom by a hanging ribbon.

Make reservations at your lover's favorite place to dine, take your balloon bouquet to the restaurant ahead of time, and set it up with management for them to have the bouquet under a bell-server when they roll the serving cart out to your table.

When the waiter approaches the table, he will lift the cover, and the balloon bouquet with your lover's anniversary or birthday gift attached will float out to be claimed.

⟨12⟩ A Christmas Time Proposal

If the Christmas season is near when you are about to ask that special someone for her hand in marriage, a unique way of proposing is to do so with a tree ornament.

You can make the tree ornament from a styrofoam ball or buy one ready made. If you make the ornament from the styrofoam ball, cut it in half and hollow out the insides. If you make it from a ready-made ornament, just take a razor blade and cut the ball in half; it will already be hollow in the middle.

Once you have done this, write a note asking if she will marry you, place it inside the ornament, tape the ball together into one piece, write on the outside, "Open up for a big surprise!" then hang the ornament on the tree for her to find.

Once the ornament is in place on the tree, your lover will read the inscription on the outside, see the tape, open up the ball, and you'll have an engagement ring for her as a Christmas gift once you get a positive answer to your proposal.

⟨13⟩ A Message Right Before Your Eyes

To leave a message right before your eyes, buy your lover a new pair of sun-glasses, or sneak their sun-glasses away when they lay them down. Then cut out two pieces of paper the size of the lens, tape it to the inside of the glasses, and on them, write the message, "I love you!" Or, "Will you marry me?" if you want to use this idea as a way to propose.

You can use a white crayon and write the message on the inside of the lens if you wish. The crayon will wipe clean from the lens once your intended has read the message and the glasses will be as good as new.

Either way, once your lover picks up the glasses to put them

11

on, the message is right before their eyes; they can't miss it.

14 *An Airport Wedding Proposal*

Tom lived in Kansas City, Janice lived in Dallas, and they were in love. The only thing that had kept them from getting married over the past two years was their jobs.

Tom was in real estate, Janice was the anchor person for a Dallas television station's nightly news program, and neither of them felt they could give up their position and relocate at that particular time.

They took turns flying to the other's home-town each weekend, Tom flying to Dallas one Friday night, Janice flying to Kansas City the next.

Each Sunday night, it got to be harder and harder to kiss and say good-bye as one of them took the other to the airport to fly back home. Finally, it got close to being impossible to do so.

Tom felt they had reached the point that if he asked Janice to marry him, she would indeed give up her job and move to Kansas City to be with him. But he loved her too much to ask or expect that of her, because he knew how much her job meant to her.

He made a decision to do something about their predicament and began to send out his resume to real estate agencies in the Dallas-Ft. Worth area that he thought might be interested in someone with his experience.

Without Janice's knowledge of what he was doing, he flew to Dallas, interviewed for a job, and got it. He flew back to Kansas City and began making plans for an airport wedding proposal for that weekend. He was to fly to Dallas. He knew Janice would be there waiting for his plane to land, so here's what he did.

He bought her a beautiful engagement ring and had it in his jacket pocket to present her when she said "yes". He bought two dozen red roses at the airport florist before he boarded the plane.

Once the plane was airborne, he told a flight-attendant what he had planned, and what the roses were for. The flight-attendant made an announcement that there was a young gentleman on the plane who planned on asking the lady of his dreams for her hand in marriage as soon as he met her at the Dallas-Ft. Worth airport, and asked if there were twenty-four volunteers who would each present his love interest one of the two dozen roses as they entered the terminal.

There were more than enough volunteers for the project at hand, and the flight attendant showed each of them a picture of Janice that Tom carried with him in his bill-fold.

When the plane landed, and the passengers disembarked, Janice was standing there just as expected to greet her lover. One by one the twenty-four volunteers presented her with a single red rose until she had a bouquet of two dozen red roses. The twenty-fifth person to come off the plane was Tom himself. He got down on one knee and said, "Janice, I love you more than life itself. I can't stand being away from you any longer. Will you marry me?"

Janice immediately said, "Yes, yes, yes!" and the crowd applauded her answer.

It was certainly a romantic wedding proposal, and needless to say, one that they will both cherish forever.

If you find yourself to be in such a situation, with your lover living in another town, you might want to try this method of asking your lover to marry you. And if you have another friend in that city as well, you might ask if they would be there, out of sight, and capture the entire happening on video so the two of you will have it to see and enjoy time and time again.

(15) Proposal Over the Airwaves

This idea depends largely on your local news coverage and how well you can sell the idea to the news director at the station. It can be on the T.V. or radio news, whichever you can manage to get it on.

If you talk to the anchor person, you can have them say, "Here is a special bulletin. Miss (your lover's name) Mr. (your name) would like to know if you will marry him."

If you talk to the weather person at the station, they can say, "Today looks like a sunny one in the life of Miss (your lovers name) because Mr. (your name) would like to know if you will marry him."

Once you have the arrangements made with your local station, be certain that you and your lover are sitting in front of the T.V. or listening to the radio (whichever you have managed to get it on) at the time of the announcement. The two of you should be together so you can see the surprise on her face, as well as get her answer to your proposal .

Most radio stations are rather easy to work with when you have a message for someone or a song dedication.

This being the case, call up the D.J. at the station who is on the air when your lover usually tunes in and ask him to dedicate a particular love song to your mate. After the D.J. has done so, he can read a message to your lover which has been prepared by you.

Some examples of the message you can write out for the D.J.

(A) "We interrupt this program to announce that John Smith would like to know if Mary Jones would marry him."
(B) "We interrupt this program to announce that Sam Jones would like to know if Susie Smith would go to dinner with him tonight."

You can use the radio message for a number of reasons. Not only is it a romantic way to propose marriage or ask that special someone out on a first date, but you can also just say, "Happy Birthday", Happy Anniversary", or, a simple "I love you!"

Once you have the plan set in motion and the D.J. is ready to dedicate the song and give your message, make certain the person to receive the message is tuned in.

Once the song and message have been aired, you can call up that special person in your life and get their response. It should be a positive one.

⑰ A Special Announcement of a Wedding Proposal

This idea actually took place in a comedy club, but you can use it at any type of nightclub, concert, etc.

What you do is talk to the M.C. or club manager and tell them what you'd like to do and what you'd like for them to say.

Then at an opportune time in the show, the M.C. or manager will come on stage, take the microphone, and announce, "Ladies and Gentlemen, we have an emergency announcement to make! Michael would like to know if Donna would marry him. Later on in the show we'll find out the answer."

Once the special announcement is made, you get your answer to your proposal and let the manager know what your love interest has decided.

In all likelihood, it will be a positive answer that you will pass on to the manager, who during the next break will again take the microphone and say, "Ladies and Gentlemen, Michael is very proud to announce his engagement to Donna, and we're very proud that this happened in our club."

⑱ Shocking Proposals

There are so many ways you can surprise your lover with a marriage proposal that you could fill an entire book with nothing else. A couple of out-of-the-ordinary proposals that were passed on to me includes the one in which a friend and his bride-to-be (as it turned out) were at a public swimming pool and my friend had the public address announcer ask her to marry him over the P.A. system for all to hear.

Another extraordinary story I heard about concerned

another friend who told me how he hid in a toll booth that his girlfriend passed each day on her drive to work. When she stopped her car to pay the toll-taker, he popped up and asked the big question.

She was at first taken by sort of a shock, but when she recovered sufficiently, her answer was in the affirmative.

I also saw a man propose marriage on national television to his unsuspecting love interest (who was viewing at home) while appearing on the Oprah Winfrey Show.

The way you choose to propose to the one you love is a personal choice that you and only you can make, but the shocking type of marriage proposals are in some cases the ones that are met with a quick answer of "YES!"

If only you put your imagination to work, you're certain to come up with the perfect way of asking for your lover's hand in marriage.

⑲ Cover Girl

After you have been together for a few years, there are lots of fond memories. Good times are a part of love and there are numerous funny little things that have happened, romantic moments the two of you have shared, etc.

With this being true in all relationships, the perfect gift for your next anniversary is to make your lover a cover girl.

To do this, take your favorite picture of your wife or girlfriend (whichever the case may be) to a novelty gift shop that puts a picture you bring in on the cover of a national magazine.

If you are married, the perfect choice would be *BRIDE MAGAZINE*. If you are only dating, you might like *COSMOPOLITAN*, *VOGUE*, or some similar women's magazine.

Have the picture put on the cover, then write several little stories about, for example, time you have shared with each other, the romantic moments, funny things she's done, trips the two of you have made together, and one about how great a person she is.

Then make up some coupons like those you see in real magazines, but these coupons will be ones your lover can redeem only through you. One can be for a new dress, one for dinner at her favorite place to dine, one for a foot rub, one for a massage, one for a night out dancing, and one for a picnic. The list could go on and on, but you should make them for things you know your mate will enjoy.

Next you take some actual advertisements from a real magazine and change the wording somewhat to suit your own purpose. For instance; if it's a Holiday Inn ad, under the last line of the advertisement you can add your own line with your love's name saying, "Come spend the weekend with us, Jill!" If it's an ad from a popular place to dine, you can add a line that makes it look as if the establishment has run an advertisement especially to ask your lover to come dine at their place of business.

Once you have the stories written and the coupons and advertisements made, take them to a type setter and have them put in the form of a real magazine. Once that's completed, have the typesetter put the magazine inside the cover you've had made at the novelty shop. Gift wrap it, then present it to your mate for an anniversary.

One last suggestion to make the gift even more special is to have on the cover, as well as in the lead story of your magazine, a heading which proclaims her WIFE OF THE YEAR! or, GIRLFRIEND OF THE YEAR!

This will be a unique gift that she'll treasure forever, show off to all her friends, and be crazy about!

20 A Special Way to Celebrate

If you live in an apartment complex or condominium, and you don't have a yard to decorate, you can use this method of decorating on an anniversary, birthday, Valentines Day, etc.

Make a large banner saying, "Happy Valentines Day", (or whatever day you're celebrating) and hang it from the railing in front of your door. Spread rose petals from your lovers parking place to your front door. You can substitute small candy kisses for the rose petals if you'd prefer. On the door, have a note saying, "Enter here for the time of your life!" or "Enter at your own risk!"

From the front door, again spread the rose petals or candy kisses leading your mate to the bathroom, where you will have a warm bath drawn and waiting, or to the bedroom, where you will be waiting with a bottle of champagne to celebrate the occasion.

If you choose to lead them to the bathroom for the warm bath, the tub should have rose petals in it as well as a few of the floating roses that you can purchase at the candle shop.

If you choose to lead them to the bedroom, you should have a romantic setting with soft lights, soft music, etc.

Whichever you choose, the warm bath or the bedroom drinks, you should have a gift-wrapped present there for them to open.

Once your lover has enjoyed the first part of the celebration, you should have their favorite meal prepared and waiting to be served in a beautiful romantic setting with soft lights and music, pretty decorations and cards befitting the occasion, whatever it is. These cards can be hand-made cards and each card should have a little message of how much your mate means to you.

You can set up the romantic dinner in the bedroom, or outside on the porch if you'd like, but the main thing is to make certain you have everything just right for an evening your mate will remember forever.

21) All Wrapped up with Wildflowers

One day, leave work a little early and gather bunches of wild flowers. Fill a plastic bag with the flowers, then, place the flowers all over your lover's car. Put them under the windshield wipers, in the cracks of the doors, gas tank lid, trunk and hood lids, and place bouquets of wildflowers on the top, hood, and trunk of the car.

Once you have the car covered with wildflowers, tie a large ribbon around the car's sides and from front to rear so that the ribbons criss-cross the car. Then attach a large postcard you can make from poster board with the message, "Happy Anniversary", Happy Birthday", or "I love you more than you will ever know!"

If you want to take the idea even further, you can have the postcard read, "We need a second honeymoon! Let's leave today." That can be your way of announcing you have made all the plans to take them on a second honeymoon.

You can use this idea to propose marriage by writing "Will you marry me?" on the postcard and taping an engagement ring to the steering wheel of the car.

22) A Surprise Wedding

After you have been married for awhile, (maybe five years or so) plan a second wedding without your wife being aware of it in advance. This is a perfect anniversary gift.

Take some time to plan it out so you don't forget any of the details. Reserve a banquet room at a very exclusive restaurant in your hometown, call up a few friends of the two of you, the preacher that actually married you, and you and your wife's family. Have them waiting in the banquet room, along with an organist and photographer, then take your wife out for an anniversary dinner.

Once the dinner is completed and you and your wife are enjoying an after dinner drink, propose marriage to her just as you did the first time. Ask if she had it to do all over if she would marry you again. When the answer is in the affirmative, say, "Then let's do it now!"

That will be the cue for the organist to begin playing the "WEDDING MARCH" and for the partition to be opened that has been concealing the guests from your wife.

You then walk to the altar (where you are joined by your best man and your wife's maid of honor) and wait as your father-in-law comes out and walks your wife down the aisle to give her away once more.

The preacher will perform the ceremony just as he did the first time, and you will have a set of rings which you have purchased as a special anniversary gift to place on her finger.

Once the ceremony has been completed, you have a nice reception planned with your friends and family, then head off on a second honeymoon with your wife.

It's for certain that this will be one anniversary the two of you will remember forever, and if you don't forget the photographer, you can have an album of the second marriage made when you return from the honeymoon (as a keepsake of the occasion).

23) Dragging Those Cans

We've all seen a newly-wedded bride and groom drive off to enjoy their honeymoon dragging those tin-cans behind the car. It's a tradition that someone tie those things to the rear bumper of the automobile, and it's a tradition that I suppose will last forever.

In fact, it's so much a tradition that the couple would

probably feel the wedding was somehow incomplete if they didn't hear the bing—bang—cling—clang as they drove away.

Well here are a couple of ideas for that old tradition, ideas that add a romantic touch and make it such a memorable occasion that the bride and groom will cherish the memory as much as the wedding itself.

Rent a hot-air-balloon and have it standing by in the parking lot just outside the place the wedding reception is held, or a nearby vacant lot if the parking lot is full of cars. When the reception reaches the point that it's time for the newly-weds to depart for their honeymoon, they get aboard the balloon and rise above the waving crowd as they take the balloon ride to the local airport, (if they are to fly to the honeymoon site) or to a location a mile or so away where their car is waiting (if they are driving to the honeymoon location).

The romance in taking the hot-air-balloon is obvious, but to add that special romantic touch, tie a long piece of strong cord to the basket of the balloon, and to the end of the cord, attach the tin-cans.

When the balloon is airborne and the happy couple are on their way, they will be dragging the traditional cans along with them and the sound of the bing—bang—cling—clang will be music to their ears.

Another romantic wedding departure that's not an everyday occurrence is to spend the wedding night in the middle of a lake on a houseboat. The following morning, the couple can depart for the regular honeymoon trip, but the first night is spent in the middle of the lake.

To get to the houseboat, the couple will depart the shore in a regular sized motor-boat, and tied to the rear of that boat will be the traditional tin-cans. The cans will of course bounce along on the water's surface, so to give them the clanging sound, place pieces of gravel inside each can. Then, place a piece of water-proof tape over the hole in the top of the cans to keep them from sinking.

This will give them the clanging sound as they bounce along behind the boat, just as they would sound if they bounced along the pavement behind the car.

㉔ A Surprise Second Honeymoon

We've all received junk mail which states we've won two nights and three days lodging at some resort area; and all we have to do to enjoy the stay is take a tour of the area to see if we would be interested in buying into a time-share program at that particular place.

You can use this idea to surprise your wife with a second honeymoon. Go to a printer and have them print up something similar to the junk mail package, then mail it to yourself.

Talk to your wife and tell her you think it would be a good idea to check into. In the meantime, make reservations at some resort. Tell them you want the honeymoon suite and have everything set up in advance.

When you and your wife arrive, there will be a candlelight dinner with champagne awaiting you in your suite. There will be a large banner hung across the bed that says, "HOPE YOU ENJOY THE SECOND HONEYMOON!" and there will be a dozen red roses for you to present your lover. You should also have a nice gift packed to surprise her with, and if you planned the second honeymoon on or near an anniversary, have some balloons which say, "HAPPY ANNIVERSARY!" hanging from the four corners of the bed.

As soon as your lover enters the room, she'll know she's been had and the whole thing was set up by you. But oh what a setup! She'll never forget it.

(25) The Boss's Anniversary Surprise

Call up your husband or wife's boss and set this one up with them just before your next wedding anniversary.

Make reservations for the weekend at a local or out of town hotel. Have the room made ready for a romantic stay with a candlelight dinner, champagne, etc. before you arrive.

Have your mate's boss call them into their office on the Friday afternoon of your anniversary weekend and say, "Happy Anniversary!" They will then hand your mate plane tickets (if you choose to go out of town) or the key to a local hotel honeymoon suite (if you're staying in town).

You will have everything packed and ready to go. When your lover comes in, the two of you are off for the anniversary surprise!

(26) Surprise Party

Call up your lover's supervisor at work and ask if you can have a surprise birthday party for your lover right there at the work site, (after work hours, of course).

If so, set it up in advance to have everything you'll need delivered to the site. Invite their work friends, and friends from outside the job as well.

Have their supervisor make up some reason they will have to work over for an hour or so on that particular day, and when everyone has arrived, have the supervisor send your lover to the area where the party is to be, using some fake reason for sending them there. When they walk in, the surprise party is waiting for them.

If the work site is not available, you can plan the party for their house, have everyone and everything waiting when they come home from work, and the surprise is just as great.

If you would rather, you can invite them to an anniversary or birthday dinner, then have all their friends waiting at the restaurant for a surprise party there.

Regardless of which place-you choose, the main thing is to keep the plans a secret from your lover so they will be truly surprised.

(27) *Sorry to wake you Honey,*
but Happy Birthday!

This is a romantic idea you can use to let your lover know you are always thinking about them. At exactly midnight on their next birthday, the minute they change age, you knock at their bedroom window. They will at first be shocked to hear the knock, but when they realize it's you, they'll open the window.

When the window is opened, you are there with a bouquet of balloons of different colors, and one heart shaped balloon that says, "Happy Birthday" on it.

You say, "I'm sorry to wake you Honey, but happy birthday!" You then give them the balloon bouquet, and if you wish, their present you have for them. You may desire to only give the balloons and save the gift for the next evening's romantic birthday dinner. But one way or the other, it's a birthday surprise your lover will enjoy.

If your lover sleeps on the second floor, it makes it even more romantic, because there are a couple of options you can add to the scheme.

You can softly toss some small pebbles against the window until you have awakened your lover. Have a long string tied to your balloon bouquet so that when they open the window, you can let the balloons fly up to them from the ground.

You can also choose to use a ladder to climb up to your lover just like in the old movies in which the leading man comes to elope with his leading lady.

(28) A Special Birthday Weekend Surprise

For a special birthday gift, leave your lover a little note where it's easily found on their birthday weekend. On the note say, "For a wonderful birthday weekend, please follow these directions. Pack these things: Toothbrush, underwear, an extra change of clothes, and your dancing shoes! I will pick you up at 7:00 P.M. tonight."

When you pick your lover up at seven, drive to a nice hotel where you have made reservations. Try to make the reservations at a place where you can enjoy a hot-tub and all the little extras.

Have a romantic dinner planned, and then as your note implied, go out and, celebrate the birthday with a night of dancing in each other's arms.

(29) To Top Off the Evening

On the next occasion you and your lover have to celebrate, be it birthday, anniversary, Valentines Day, etc., after you have given your gift and enjoyed a romantic dinner together, top the evening off with a unique surprise for your lover.

To do this, take a roll of wide red ribbon and criss-cross the bed with it. Tie the ribbon in a big bow in the middle of the bed (so it looks as if the bed is gift wrapped) and place a dozen red roses, two glasses, and a bottle of champagne under the bow.

Have everything in place before you depart home for the romantic dinner, including several candles spread throughout the bedroom.

When you return home, light the candles, then say, "And now to top off the evening!" as you escort your lover into the bedroom. The unique surprise is there awaiting them and you have topped off the evening with one last romantic notion.

30 Spell It Out With Kisses

Buy a few bags of the small candy kisses, (or as many bags as it takes to write the note you want to leave) and write your lover a note on the sidewalk leading to their house, on the front porch, or some place where they will easily discover your message.

If you leave the candy kiss love note outside, make certain to leave it just before they are due to arrive, (so the candy doesn't melt from the sun) or on a cool day.

You can write your love note and say whatever you'd like by laying the small kisses side by side to form the letters; here are a few examples of messages:

(A) "HAPPY BIRTHDAY HONEY!"
(B) "HAPPY ANNIVERSARY! I'LL LOVE YOU FOREVER!"
(C) "WILL YOU MARRY ME CONNIE? FROM DON."
(D) "I'M ABOUT TO DIE FOR A KISS! WHAT ABOUT YOU?"
(E) "THIS IS FOR ALL THOSE TIMES I FORGOT TO GIVE YOU A KISS!"

31 Birthday Music

If you play a musical instrument, you may want to try this idea for a surprise gift for your lover's next birthday.

If you write music and lyrics, write an original love song for your lover. If you don't write, hire someone who does to write the score sheet and lyrics for you. Then gift wrap the instrument you play as well as the lead sheet of the love song in a box for them to open.

Have a tape recorder ready, and when your lover opens the gift, turn on the recorder, take out the instrument, and play the original love song to them.

The lyrics to the song should express exactly how you feel about your lover. So after you've played your birthday song, you give them the tape recording of it as a present they can keep forever to remember the moment by.

Your lover will play it time and again, and each time, the song will mean so much to them.

(32) Piano-Bars

A piano-bar is a marvelous setting as a place to give your lover a romantic message. There are several ways to accomplish this; here are a few ideas:

(A) If you have the talent for it, you can write a love song for your mate and pay the piano player to dedicate the song, announce that you wrote the song for your lover, then sing the song to them.

(B) If you don't have the capabilities to write your own love song, see the piano player a few days ahead of time and pay him to write a love song for you and-your mate, then on the night you visit the bar, he can dedicate the song to the both of you and sing it.

(C) If you have a good voice, you can sing the song to your lover yourself while the piano player accompanies you.

(D) You can request a particular song that your mate loves to hear. When the piano player goes into the song, you can have flowers delivered to your mate at your table.

You may wish a simple song like "HAPPY BIRTHDAY TO YOU" on your mate's birthday and have a cake with candles brought to your table on their next birthday.

You can also propose marriage in this setting by requesting a suitable song for the occasion and taking out the engagement ring and asking the big question at just the right time.

CHAPTER TWO
GIFTS AND PROPS

Giving gifts to the one you love is something you just want to do when you're in love. To the true romantic, the old saying that, "It is better to give than receive" is as true a statement as there has ever been. The true romantic has a passion for showering his lover with gifts. This chapter gives you ideas on special gifts, ways to give them, and even prop gifts to make your lover feel good all over about the fact that you are so much in love with them.

(33) How do I love Thee?
Let me count the Ways

It's always good to reassure your mate that you do indeed love them. Of course, actions speak louder than words, but the words themselves are nice to hear and are an added bonus to your actions that your lover wants, as well as needs to hear from you.

A fantastic way to say "I love you" is to compile a list of all the reasons why you do and give it to your lover. The list is a personal thing and each of us has different reasons why we are in love with that special person, but some ideas for your list can include the way they always show you that they love you too, how they always seem to understand and accept your different moods, the way they smell, walk, talk, the color of their eyes, hair, the way they make you laugh, and how comfortable it makes you feel just knowing they're there for you. The list can go on and on, and the more reasons you have, the better.

Once you have made your list, the way you present it to your lover is up to you. You can write a letter with all the reasons included, put it in an envelope, and place it under their pillow, where they are sure to find it.

You can make a little game of it by writing each reason on a separate postcard and hiding them around the house (such as in the cookie-jar) for them to find.

Instead of hiding the postcards, you can mail them one a day, and stretch it out for as long as you have reasons to send, or mail them all at once in a small decorative box.

If your mate works in an office with a fax-machine, you can fax your reasons to them while they're on the job. That will be sure to make their day.

If you prefer to make a gift of your list, you can:

(A) Put all your reasons in a nice card and have it delivered with a flower arrangement.

(B) Type the reasons on different colors of paper, cut them out, wrap the ends of the cut-outs around toothpicks, then tape them to make little flags. Stick the toothpick flags all over a nice flower arrangement and have it delivered.

(C) Buy your lover a box of individually wrapped candy mints.

30

Unwrap each piece, and instead of making flags from the typed out reasons, place the different colored papers inside the mints wrappers , replace the mints, wrap them then once more, put them back in the box, gift wrap the candy box and have it delivered to your lover. As they eat each piece, they will discover another reason why you love them.

(D) If you have the talent for it, write a song or poem about all the reasons you're in love. If it's a song, make a tape recording and give them the tape as a gift.

If it's a poem, type out the poem, put it in a nice picture frame, (so it can be set on a table or hung on a wall) gift wrap it, and give it to your lover over a romantic dinner.

34 The Ultimate Gift

Larry was an imaginative romantic who truly loved Sherry. Larry had given Sherry all types of gifts over the years and was lost as to what he would give her for Christmas.

He purchased several typical items, gift wrapped them, and had them under the tree for her to open Christmas morning. To a romantic such as-Larry, this just didn't seem to be enough, and he had always presented Sherry with something special on every special occasion. He had run out of ideas for these types of gifts until he suddenly realized the one most important gift he could ever give her was himself.

He had certainly given of himself! He had given his love, time, devotion, and all the things necessary to make their relationship one of true happiness. Then he decided to give himself in the literal sense to point out the fact that he was indeed hers in the figurative sense.

On Christmas Eve night Larry went to a local store and got a large cardboard box that he could fit into. He then had two friends gift wrap the box once he was inside, and on Christmas

Eve night, the two friends carried the box with Larry inside to Sherry (who was waiting at home, thinking Larry was out doing some last minute shopping).

The card which was given Sherry by the delivery men said, "To the woman I love more than life itself. I have given you every gift I thought you would enjoy, and now I give you the ultimate gift. Please open as soon as you receive this package, for this gift is one that you should have all for your own. Open it in private, and keep it dear to your heart forever. Love, Larry."

As soon as Sherry tore open the box, there was Larry himself in his birthday suit. Sherry immediately knew exactly what the present represented and knew the meaning was that Larry was indeed hers forever, to keep, cherish, and love more than any material gift he could ever give her.

That Christmas Eve night was one that will always be special to both Larry and Sherry, and the ultimate gift is one Sherry does indeed treasure more than any gift she has ever or could ever receive.

You can give the ultimate gift to your lover in various ways. You can give yourself on a birthday, anniversary, Christmas, or just have the present delivered on a normal day as a special surprise. You can have someone wrap you in gift wrapping without the box and lay you on the bed, place you under the Christmas tree, or anywhere you like. If you're placed on the bed, have rose petals strewn from the door to the bed itself so your lover will follow the trail when they arrive home. If you're placed under the Christmas tree, make sure you are placed there only ten minutes or so before your lover is due to open presents.

The card attached should be a personal message from you to your lover and can say whatever you would like, but be sure and say this is the ultimate gift when enclosing your message.

So go ahead and have yourself gift wrapped and delivered. It will be the one present your lover will cherish forever.

35 *Invitation to Imitation*

If your lover absolutely adores a particular actor, singer, or other well known celebrity (even someone from the past such as Clark Gable), send them a picture of that person. On the picture write, "I can't wait to see you for dinner tonight!" Then sign the name of the celebrity.

Have your hair done in the style the celebrity wears and dress as they do. Make yourself look as much like that person as possible. If it's someone from out of the past, a costume rental company may be your best bet. You can rent the costume to look even more like the person.

If not, then you'll have to use your own imagination and put together your own outfit.

When you show up for dinner, use the mannerisms of the person you are portraying, try to talk as they do, and your lover will have a ball as they enjoy your little show.

A very romantic way to show your love, as well as your thoughtfulness, is to give your lover a true-love coupon book.

Make the book yourself by taking three-by-five file cards (or something similar) and cut them into the shape of a heart. Take a hole-punch, make a hole in the upper left part of the heart, and attach them by placing a red ribbon through the holes. You can curl the ends of the ribbon to make it more attractive, then present the coupon book to your lover in any way you desire.

You can gift wrap it and leave it where they will find it with a note saying, "To the one I love", you can have it delivered to their work site or home by a delivery man, or you can present the gift to them in person over a romantic dinner with a bottle of champagne.

The coupons are redeemable upon presentation and the book should say so on the front. What that means is as soon as your lover presents one of the coupons to you, you have to deliver whatever the coupon calls for with no excuses. If there is something you don't want to do, you had better not make a coupon for it.

There can be as many coupons as you would like and you can use your own imagination when making them.

Some examples are a coupon for a picnic, one for a new dress, one for the movie of their choice, one for a night out dancing, dinner at their favorite restaurant, a back rub, foot rub, or massage. The possibilities are limitless and you can make them for what your lover enjoys.

Just remember, you have to deliver when they present the coupon, so make a book that you'll both enjoy and have a good time with it.

The woman who stays home to keep the children, keep house, and make sure the family is cared for in the proper way has a thankless job, (or so it seems to them at times) though it's the most important job one could ever imagine.

There is no question that the person needs a break from the kids on occasion, so one week, on a Thursday, have a dozen roses delivered to her (this gives her time to look forward to what's in store for her) and attached to the bouquet of roses, have two coupons decorated with curled ribbons (which you have made yourself).

The first coupon will say, "This coupon is for a new outfit." With the self-made coupon you will attach a gift certificate from one of the better clothing stores in your town.

Coupon number two will have a small envelope attached to it. The coupon will say, "This coupon is for a free weekend just for you to do as you wish! I'll keep the kids and clean the house." Inside the envelope you will place a one hundred-dollar bill for her to spend as she wishes.

Send a nice card with the flowers and coupons, and on the card write, "I realize how tough it must be doing the fantastic job you do with the house and children, and I want you to know how much I appreciate it."

Then say the free weekend is up at 5:00 P.M. on Sunday night because you have a special surprise lined up for her.

The special surprise will be that you have a baby-sitter lined up for the evening and reservations at a nice restaurant for a romantic dinner for two.

Don't forget, the weekend is a free one for her, so you prepare and serve her breakfast in bed on both Saturday and Sunday mornings. Take care of the children all weekend (until the sitter arrives Sunday evening) and have the house clean as a pin. You can clean it yourself or hire it done, but it should look just as good as it does when she herself does it.

Buying your lover an expensive gift is not an everyday happening in most cases. The gift itself is proof of how much you love and care for your mate, but you can make it even more special (as well as romantic) by taking it just one step further.

Say your lover has seen a new car that they want very badly, so you go out and buy them the car for a birthday, Christmas, or anniversary present. Instead of just driving up and announcing that you bought them the car, you can gift wrap the car keys to present to your lover, and tie a big ribbon around the car itself.

Tie a ribbon from front to rear bumper, and from side to side around the body of the car, coming into a large bow on top of the car.

Give them the gift-wrapped keys, and once opened, take your lover to the garage or driveway (wherever you've hidden the car) and announce, "It's all yours!"

The same is true when a couple is looking for that first house. Once your mate has found that home of their dreams, you can close the deal with the realtor without your mate's knowledge of it. If they have to sign the papers on the house, the realtor will be happy to let them sign later (after you have given your lover the surprise of their life).

Once the deal is closed, go to a florist and buy a large roll of wide red ribbon. Tie the ribbon around the outside of the house, and make a big bow on the front door. Gift wrap the front door key and have it inside a jacket pocket. Ask your mate if they would like to drive out and look at the house one more time, and when you drive up, they'll see the gift-wrapped home of their dreams. You take out the gift-wrapped key, present it to them, and say, "It's all yours!"

They'll love it!

(39) The Big Game

Ladies, if your man is really into sports, for an extra special surprise gift, purchase two tickets to a big sporting event that's coming up (such as a World Series Game, Super Bowl, Heavyweight Boxing Championship, etc.).

Make hotel reservations in the city hosting the event, purchase round-trip plane tickets to the city, then give them over a romantic dinner.

Tell him he can take anyone he would like with him to enjoy the big game (such as his best friend) and that you just want him to enjoy himself.

If you're lucky, he'll choose to take you along on the second ticket. But, if he takes you literally and takes an old buddy, don't be hurt over his decision! After all, it is a sporting event and you want him to enjoy it. That's the whole idea behind the gift.

If you find you have problems getting tickets to events like the World Series, you can check the local schedule of games which might be coming up. Your local college football team is certain to have a big rivalry on their schedule. Your man would want to attend that for sure, and the tickets would not be that hard to secure.

(40) The Spontaneous Love Gift

The next time you are out shopping with your lover, say you have to look for something, excuse yourself from them for a moment, then go to the card section and pick out a lovely card saying how much they mean to you. Go to the flower section of the supermarket, or the florist if you are in a shopping mall, and get a dozen roses or a bouquet of their favorite flowers.

Once you have signed the card and have the flowers in hand, approach your lover right there in the store and give them your spontaneous love gift. It will both surprise and thrill them to know you do love them and have them on your mind at all times.

(41) Presents from out of the Blue

Buy your lover a lot of presents and give them on a regular day. These presents will not be for a birthday, anniversary, or any other special day. They will be given for no other reason than to say "I love you".

On the day you pick to shower your lover with all these unexpected gifts, get up early, serve them breakfast in bed, then present them the first gift. This gift can be something like a ring, necklace, or some other piece of jewelry.

While they are enjoying their breakfast, draw them a warm bath. While the bath is being drawn, fill the bathroom with flowers. You can purchase the flowers the evening before and keep them in your car overnight (they will still be fresh that morning).

After the warm bath, present your lover with the next present. This one can be a new-outfit for them to wear to work that day.

While your lover is at work, have the next present delivered to them on the job. This present can be anything you decide they might enjoy.

When your lover returns home from work, have the next present laid out waiting for them-on the bed, gift-wrapped. Spread rose petals from the doorway to the bedroom to give them a trail to follow to this gift.

The gift can be another outfit and the outfit should be something from the evening~wear line so they can change into it for a special romantic dinner out that night.

After dinner, have another present to give your lover over drinks. This gift should be small in size so you can have it in your pocket during the dinner. It can be a gold broach, a small bottle of perfume, or something along those lines.

When you return home for the evening, present your lover the last gift of the day. This gift should be a sexy nightgown or negligee your lover can wear to bed right-then.

These gifts are only ideas and you can substitute your own for any of these. The main-thing is to plan this on a regular day and give gifts you know your lover will enjoy. No matter what the gifts, your lover is sure to enjoy the romantic notion behind them all and will treasure the cards and messages you have given with each.

(42) A Love Gift

Sending flowers, candy, perfume, or gifts such as these on special occasions is usually expected of us. What is really special is the gift that's not anticipated by your lover and is given to them out of the blue.

You can show up unexpectedly either at their place of work, or their house on your lunch break and give them your gift on what would otherwise be an ordinary day. You give the gift for no other reason than to show your love for them.

This is the perfect way to say, "I love you, and you're always on my mind."

One romantic gift your lover is sure to treasure is a gold key necklace.

Go to a jewelry store, buy a gold key, place the key on a gold chain so it can hang around the neck of your mate, then give them the gift over a romantic dinner.

Another gift which is similar in thought and just as certain to please is half a gold coin.

Have a gold coin cut in half and have both halves put on gold chains so you and your lover both have half a gold coin to wear.

Whichever gift you choose, you should have the small box containing the necklace gift wrapped and place a single rose under the bow and ribbon. Pick out a suitable card and write your message, saying something like, "You hold the key to my happiness", or, "You have the key to my heart and you are the only owner."

If you decide on the half coin as a gift, you can say, "We are the only two that fit together," or, "Without you, I'm only half a person."

You can give these gifts on a birthday or anniversary, but it's best to give them on an otherwise ordinary day; then the meaning of the gift sinks in and makes the giving and receiving a little more romantic.

44 *Something Precious*

On an ordinary day, when your lover isn't expecting anything from you, give them a gift of gold. Anything gold will do. It can be a chain for their neck, an anklet for their ankle, a ring, gold watch, earrings, etc.

Have the present gift-wrapped, and with it have a nice card which says, "Gold is precious, but only half as precious as you!"

You could do this on a birthday, anniversary, etc. But it's best to give it on an ordinary day just to let them know they are indeed the most precious thing in your life and that you're always thinking of them. On an ordinary day, the gift just has a little more meaning to your lover.

On a day that's usually spent with your wife cleaning house, hire a cleaning service to come in and do the job for her.

Set everything up in advance and when the rent-a-maid shows up ringing the door-bell, it will be a complete surprise to your wife.

The maid will hand her a card from you saying how much you love her and how you appreciate everything she does for you. Inside the envelope you will have placed the following gift certificates: One for a hair styling, one for a facial, one for a manicure, and all from a local salon. You will also have put in one for a new dress from one of the finer clothing stores in town, one for a new pair of shoes from a local shoe store, and also enclosed will be at least a fifty-dollar bill for some spending money (even more if you would like).

If you have children at an age when they must be attended to, also enclose a gift certificate for a day at the day care close by your home.

Your closing message on your card will say, "Meet me at 6:00 P.M. (at the place you have made reservations) for a romantic dinner. Hope you have a fantastic day!"

The two of you will meet to have the romantic dinner, enjoy the evening together, and it will be a day she will never forget. She will know for certain that you do indeed love her and appreciate all she does.

(46) A Remedy for A Bad Day

The next time your mate leaves for work in a bad mood, for whatever reason, help remedy the bad day by sending them a balloon-o-gram, flowers, perfume, candy, or some suitable gift, with a card from you saying, "I know you're having a bad day, but no matter how bad the day seems, you know I love you and am thinking of you."

You can send a singing telegram with the message that you hope this brightens up their day, or you can send a gift by someone dressed as a clown with a card saying, "The day is not that bad! Look on the bright side, and the bright side is that I love you and I'm here waiting to make your day better as soon as you return."

You can also use this idea to make up with your lover after a disagreement by stating on the card how sorry you are about the argument.

(47) A Gift at Work

Buy your mate a nice gift, gift wrap the box, attach a card with your message, then have it delivered to their place of work.

The gift and message can be several different things, such as, a lovely new dress with the message, "Wear this tonight when you meet me for dinner." Then you tell them the time and place they are to meet you.

You might like to send tickets to a play your lover has been wanting to see and the message can say, "Meet me for a lovely evening." Then tell them the time and place they're to meet you for the two of you to see the play together.

There are limitless possibilities for your gift and message, and your lover is certain to enjoy a gift sent from out of the blue no matter what you send as the gift.

48 A Surprise Among the Papers

If your lover's job requires tons of paperwork, and they have to bring the paperwork home with them at times, slip in a little surprise!

Late one night after they have finished with the paper work and called it an evening, slip into their briefcase, take out the work they are involved in, and slip a sexy picture in among the papers. A picture of yourself in a sexy nightgown, a French cut bathing suit, or a tiny cut bikini would be perfect.

Along with the picture, leave a note that says, "I can't wait till you get home!" Or, "I love you so much!"

When they get to the office and start going over the previous night's work, they'll find the note and picture and it's certain to brighten their day.

You can use this idea as a way of announcing a surprise vacation or weekend getaway by placing airline tickets to the place you are going inside the paperwork with a note saying, "Get ready to have a great time! We leave this afternoon as soon as you're home and packed!"

(49) Newspaper Delivery

To give your lover a big surprise, when the newspaper is delivered, get to it before they do. In their favorite section of the paper (the section they turn to first) place a nice card to your lover with a message from you, as well as a gift.

The card can say whatever you'd like, such as, "I love you! Or, "Thank you for marrying me. It made my life complete!"

The gift can be plane tickets for the two of you to take a vacation together, a gift certificate for a new dress, tickets to a ballgame, play, concert, movie, etc., or, just a single rose.

The card and gift can also be placed inside the paper as a thank-you note for something special they have done for you. If you would like, it can be a thank-you note for nothing in particular (just to let your lover know you think of them always) such as "Thank you for the great time last night!"

Whatever the reason you leave the card and gift, your lover will cherish the thought.

(50) Postcards

Make your own postcard by taking a piece of poster board, folding it in half, writing your message to your lover inside, then taking a large picture of yourself (an eight-by-ten will do) and glue or tape it to the front of the card.

Take some white gift wrapping paper and fold it in the shape of an envelope. Make a large stamp from a piece of paper about the size of a sheet of note-book paper, (drawing the figures on the stamp yourself) and glue it in the upper right hand corner of the envelope you have made.

Place the postcard inside and have it delivered to your lover. A taxi driver will deliver it for you, but if you prefer the real mail service, you can take it to the Post Office where they will weigh the card and stamp the postage on it, then deliver it through the regular mail.

(51) *The Fax of Love*

Ladies, if you want to really make your lover eager to get home to you after work, buy yourself a new sexy nightgown, have a friend take a picture of you in your new outfit, then fax the picture to your lover at work.

Send a note with the picture saying, "When you get home, I'll be waiting as I am!" It's for certain he won't be late coming in!

If your lover is out of town on a business trip, take a real nice picture of a dozen roses and fax the picture to him with a note saying how much you love and miss him and can't wait till he gets home.

(52) *A Sexy Card*

There are all sorts of occasions on which we send our lover a card, and sometimes we choose to send them a sexy one. You've seen all types of sexy greeting cards in the card store, but a personal one would have extra meaning to your lover.

Next time you send your lover a greeting card, make it just that sexy and personal!

To do this, have a picture made of yourself in a negligee, bikini underwear, or anything sexy. Write a sexy message for it, or copy one from a store-bought card, then take it to a print shop. Have them make a real card, one just like the ones you would normally buy, print the message on the inside, and instead of the regular picture of a professional model on the front, put your picture there.

Your lover will think more of this card than any you could ever purchase at the card store!

A good way to keep an affair or marriage from going stale is to send a message which gets right to the point, says something romantic, and uses a prop to get to that point.

This should be done on an ordinary day, just out of the blue, at a time when your lover isn't expecting anything from you.

Some examples of the props you can use are a giant-sized candy kiss, several small candy kisses, a box or can of mixed nuts or cashews, or the small heart-shaped red hot cinnamon candy pieces.

You can have the prop delivered or hand deliver it yourself. If you choose to have it delivered, have it gift wrapped with a nice card conveying your message.

For instance, if you send the giant kiss, say, "There is no greater kiss in the world than yours."

If you send several of the small kisses, you can say, "There is no limit to how far I would go for your kisses."

If you send the nuts, say, "I'm completely nuts about you!"

If you send the small cinnamon hearts, you can say, "My heart is burning with the desire to be close to you."

You may want to use your own imagination and come up with your own little props, and you can write a suitable message to go along with it; but make the message short, sweet, and to the point, just to let them know you do indeed love them and they are on your mind.

(54) A Picture Collage

One gift your wife or husband is certain to treasure is a collage of pictures of the two of you together. If you have been married five or fifty-years, it matters not; you're sure to have lots of pictures of the two of you together stashed away somewhere.

Get them out of those drawers, put them together in chronological order, have them placed in a nice frame, gift wrap it, and give it as a birthday, anniversary, valentines Day present, or just as a special gift that says "I love you!"

As I said, it's a gift your lover will cherish forever.

(55) Love in Art

Take a picture of your lover to a local artist and have them do a life-size painting of your mate. Or take it to a sculptor and have them sculpt a bust of your lover.

If you possess these talents, you can draw or sculpt it yourself.

Once you have a completed project, gift wrap it and give it as a present. It is an artistic gift they will be sure to want and have probably wished to have for some time but never wanted to take the time to pose for it.

It's a present your lover will forever cherish and you will as well; in fact you may want to do two of them, or have two of them done so you can keep one for yourself.

(56) Homemade T.V. Show

A nice gift for an upcoming birthday or anniversary is a homemade video T.V. show.

Take lots of old videos you've made over the years, or old home movies and have them converted over to video tape, then act as the narrator as you talk about what each scene is and what makes the event special in the life of your mate.

For example, use old movies or videos of the two of you on an outing to the mountains, beach, a picnic, family reunion, etc.

You can use old shots of the children and put them in proper order, (showing them growing up) then at the end of the video, you can act as interviewer and ask each child what makes their Mother or Father (whichever the video is being made for) the special person they are to them.

After the children's interviews, you then give all the reasons why you are truly in love with your mate.

You can also make part of the HOMEMADE T.V. SHOW a comedy by editing the film and asking questions of your mate that makes what they said years ago hysterically funny. For an example, if, in the original film, your mate was talking about the food she had packed for a family picnic, and she said, "We had better eat; the food is getting cold and it won't be any good." You can ask the question, "How would you like to go to my Mother's this weekend and eat Sunday dinner?"

Then you edit out part of what she said at the picnic to make her answer to your question, "Eat! The food won't be any good!" By taking out the "We had better is getting cold and it", you make it look as if she can't stand your Mother's cooking.

There are all kinds of possibilities in editing the old film to make your new video funny, and it's a special gift that your mate will long cherish.

(57) You Can Be A Star

If you're musically inclined and have the ability to write a love song, write one for your lover. If you play an instrument (such as a guitar or piano) so much the better.

If you have these talents, go to a local studio and record the song for your lover. There are small studios which offer this service to people in most all larger cities.

If you prefer, you can rent a video camera (if you don't own one) and make a video of you performing the song just like the big stars you see on M.T.V.

If you don't possess these talents, you can write a poem saying how much you love and care for them and make a video of you reciting the poem to them.

Give the recording or video to your lover as a gift that they can enjoy forever and play or show to their friends.

(58) You Are the D.J.

Make a tape of old love songs and songs that will bring back fond memories for your lover when they hear them. Then you become the D.J. as you introduce each song on the tape just as they would do on a radio show.

You can record songs like "I WANT TO HOLD YOUR HAND" and in your introduction to the song, you can say how you love holding their hand when the two of you are out in public.

You can record the old love song "I ONLY HAVE EYES FOR YOU" and tell them how they are the only one in the world you will ever love.

You'll need to record some of the songs which the two of you listened to and which were popular when the two of you first met. Be sure to express what memory in particular each song brings back to you.

Make your introduction to each song as romantic as possible and choose songs with lyrics which express how you feel about your lover.

Once you have made the tape, put it in the tape player of their car. Attach a note to their steering wheel saying, "Hope you enjoy the music I've chosen for you. I love you."

Your lover is sure to enjoy the tape and it will become a keepsake they will cherish forever.

59 A Unique Way to Give A Dozen Roses

The next time you decide to give your lover a dozen roses, give them in a way you have never presented them before by using this method.

Take eleven flowers and spread them through the house with a note attached to each rose for your lover to find.

The last rose you will place on your lover's chest so they will discover it first when they awaken. The rose will be wrapped in green flower paper with babies breath, and the note with it can say, "A ROSE FOR A ROSE!" Or, "I LOVE WAKING UP NEXT TO SOMEONE AS SEXY AS YOU!"

Rose number two can be placed on the nightstand, and the note can say, "I'M SO LUCKY TO HAVE SOMEONE AS WONDERFUL AS YOU!"

Rose number three can be placed on the bathroom door-knob with a note saying, "IT'S SO GREAT WAKING UP WITH SOMEONE AS PRETTY AS YOU!"

Rose number four can be taped to the bathroom mirror, and the note attached will say, "SEE! WHAT DID I TELL YOU? YOU

ARE SO PRETTY!"

Rose number five will be placed in the shower with a note saying, "THIS ROSE IS FOR ALL THE TIMES WE'VE MADE LOVE AND IT FELT AS IF I WAS IN HEAVEN!"

Rose number six is hidden under a folded towel with a note saying, "THIS IS FOR ALL THE TIMES I SHOULD HAVE SAID I WAS SORRY AND FAILED TO SAY IT!"

Rose number seven is placed on the closet door. Or, you can lay out the clothes they are to wear that day and lay the flower and note with them. You may want to buy them a new outfit to lay out with the rose with a note saying, "THIS ROSE IS IN CASE I FORGOT ONE, I'M SORRY!"

Rose number eight will be placed inside the shoes they are to wear with a note saying, "I JUST WANT TO SAY I'M SORRY BEFORE I MESS UP THE NEXT TIME. SO I'M SORRY!"

Rose number nine will be taped to the refrigerator door with a note which says, "I JUST LOVE YOU FOR BEING YOU!"
Rose number ten will be on the inside of the front door of the house (so they will find it as they are leaving) and the note with it will say, "THIS ROSE IS BECAUSE WITHOUT YOU IN MY LIFE, THERE WOULD BE NO LOVE IN MY LIFE!"

Rose number eleven will be placed on the car door handle or placed in the seat of their car with a note saying, "I SURE HOPE YOU HAVE A ROSEY DAY!"

The last rose of the dozen will be delivered to your lover during the day by a special carrier and the note with it will say, "I CAN'T WAIT TO SEE YOU AT HOME TONIGHT! I HAVE A SPECIAL SURPRISE LINED UP FOR YOU!"

The surprise you have waiting can be you waiting with a bottle of champagne and dressed in the sexiest outfit ever imagined. Or, you may wish to have a romantic dinner waiting for them.

The surprise can be anything you know for certain your lover would enjoy; in any case, the way you presented the roses, and the surprise at the end of the day will insure that your lover will never forget this day in your lives.

This idea is also an excellent way for a man to say how much he cares for the woman who is expecting his child, and the woman expecting may really need to hear these things at that time in her life.

If you are married, or if you have been dating someone for awhile, their favorite things are obvious to you. You know their favorite place to dine, favorite song, movie, flowers, color, etc.

If you're interested in someone you haven't been out with, you must first find out a couple of these things before setting this plan in motion. Find out what their favorite type flower and favorite color is, then go to work.

If their favorite flower is a rose, and their favorite color is red for example, no problem; you send them a dozen red roses. But, say their favorite color is purple? Then you have to improvise.

To send that special someone a bouquet of purple roses, you can go to the florist a day in advance and ask them to dye the roses for you, or you can buy a box of regular dye, mix it in your sink, submerge the roses for a few minutes, and make them yourself.

If you're in a big hurry to give the flowers, then you can spray paint the flowers the color you desire, allow them to dry for about thirty minutes, and they're ready.

The idea behind this is to make certain it is the favorite type flower and the favorite color of that special someone you have in mind, so if that particular flower doesn't come natural in that color, you can certainly make a lasting impression by coming up with the perfect colored bouquet.

(61) *One Week's Worth of Flowers*

Once a day for seven days, have a single flower delivered to your lover. Each flower should be a different type, and with the flower, there should be a nice card with your message on it.

Each card can have a different reason why you love them, or say why that particular flower, or color of it, reminds you of them.

In place of the card, you can send a short love letter with the flower saying some of the things you have meant to say for some time but just haven't gotten around to it.

We're all guilty of that, and this idea is the perfect format for saying those things we really want to say to our lover.

(62) *Two Dozen Roses*

On the next occasion you are sending your lover flowers, instead of the normal dozen roses, add an extra touch by sending them two dozen roses with an attached card which says, "Double the roses for double the love I have for you!"

You can also propose marriage a second time and even suggest a second honeymoon by putting on the card, "The second time around should be twice as much fun! Will you marry me again?"

Your lover will appreciate the gesture and get the message that they mean twice as much to you as anyone else ever could. They'll love it!"

63 Wild Flowers Along the Road

The next time you and your lover are driving along and you spot some wild flowers along the roadside, stop the car, get out, (without saying a word) and pick a bouquet of wild flowers for your lover. Give it to them and say, "I love you more than you could ever know!" Give them a gentle kiss, then continue your drive.

Your lover will be impressed by the small act and feel good about the love the two of you have for each other.

64 Roses at Dinner

Set this one up with the waiter at your lover's favorite place to dine on the day you are to take your mate there for a romantic evening.

Have the waiter deliver your lover roses just before the two of you are served the meal. There are several ways to have the roses delivered:

(A) A dozen roses are on the reserved table when you are seated with a card from you saying how much you are in love.

(B) The waiter delivers the roses as he serves your drinks with a card from you on a silver platter.

(C) Eleven roses are on the table when you're seated and the waiter delivers the card from you which says, "The twelfth rose is you, and you are the most beautiful of all.

(D) Eleven roses are on the table when you are seated and the waiter delivers a single yellow rose with a card from you which says, "You are the yellow rose, the one that's different from all the rest, and the one I love the best!"

You can use this idea as a way of proposing marriage by having eleven roses on the table when you are seated and the waiter brings out the twelfth rose with the engagement ring around its stem. He presents the rose and ring to your lover on a silver platter, and as he does, you ask your lover if she will marry you.

65 A Tricky Surprise with Flowers

If one of your neighbors has a nice flower garden that your lover adores, talk to the neighbor in advance (so they will know what you're up to). See what kind of flowers they have in bloom, then go to the florist and buy some just like them.

Once you have done this hide the flowers you have purchased some place in your neighbor's garden. As you and your lover are driving by, stop the car in front of the neighbor's house, run to the garden as if you are stealing the flowers, find your bouquet you've hidden earlier, run back to the car as if you're afraid of getting caught, present your lover the flowers, say, "I love you", then speed off as if you're trying to get out of sight.

Your lover will at first be shocked by your bold and daring move, so let them feel the shock for awhile. Then confess what you have done. Your lover will enjoy the joke, and more importantly, they'll enjoy the bouquet.

66 Roses are Dead, Violets are Blue

Sending flowers to your partner is certainly romantic, and almost even commonplace. Where the true romantic captures the heart is by taking the ordinary and taking it one step beyond. To be a true romantic, use your imagination! For instance, take the sending of the flowers and go one step further. Send a dozen roses , but send dead ones with one of the following notes.

If the person is someone you are attracted to and wish to see, attach a note saying, "I'm dying to go out with you!"

If you're out of town, have the note read, "I'm dying to get back to you!" Or, "I'm dying to get home to see you!"

It's out of the ordinary, it's romantic, and it's sure to capture the heart!

(67) Your Surprise Birthday

It is common practice to send flowers on a birthday, but a romantic twist to the old idea is to send your lover flowers on YOUR birthday instead of their own.

On YOUR birthday, have the flowers delivered to your lover with a card saying, "Thanks for being there whenever I needed you", or, "Without you in my life, I wouldn't want to get any older."

Another romantic message is "As I grow older, my love for you grows stronger!" You can combine the messages by saying, "As I get older, my love for you gets better and better, and without you in my life I wouldn't want to grow older."

The message you send can be a personal one from you to your lover, but the idea is to send the flowers on YOUR birthday so it will be a complete surprise.

(68) Thanks Mom!

This idea is good if your lover is very close to their Mother, or if they are still living in their parent's home.

Send a dozen roses with a beautiful card attached, but instead of having them delivered to your love interest, send them to their Mother.

On the card, say, "Thank you for having the (girl or man) of my dreams!" Or, "Thank you for having the only (girl or man) I could ever be in love with!"

The Mother will appreciate the thought, and your lover will be delighted with the fact that you took the time to thank their Mother for bringing them into the world.

69 A Balloon-o-gram

Send a balloon-o-gram to your lover at their place of work or to their home if you'd prefer. Attached to the balloon-o-gram, and hanging from the bottom, you can send:

(A) Tickets to a ballgame your lover wants to attend.

(B) Tickets to a play or movie they have been wanting to see.

(C) Tickets to a concert or opera they've been wanting to hear.

(D) Airline tickets for an out of town trip for the two of you to enjoy.

(E) A bottle of champagne decorated with curled ribbons with a card which says, "Happy Birthday", "Happy Anniversary", etc.

(F) Just a love letter telling them how much you love and need them.

(G) You may choose to combine these ideas and send tickets to one of the above things your lover has wanted to do, (except to an out-of-town ballgame, concert, etc). If the event is out of town, you also attach the plane tickets for the two of you.

One day when they least expect anything out of the ordinary from you, go to your lovers work place, find their car, and surprise them by decorating it with balloons. Not just a few balloons, but balloons galore.

Write a short message with a magic marker on each balloon, such as, "I love you", "Can we have dinner tonight?" "You are the most beautiful person I have ever seen!" Or, use this idea to give your lover a list of all the reasons you do love them by putting a different reason on each balloon.

Once you have written a message on enough balloons to completely decorate the automobile, tie the balloon to the bumpers, gas cap, antenna, windshield wipers, and hood ornament, then fill the inside of the car with the balloons, leaving just enough room for them to sit and drive.

You can use this idea to propose marriage by writing, "Will you marry me?" on some of the balloons, and "I love you" on the others.

You may also use this idea to celebrate a special day by writing, "Happy birthday", Happy anniversary", etc. on the balloons.

If you wish, you can use this same idea, but be a little less extravagant, by using a single balloon and writing your message on it.

(71) A Gift Along the Trail

Sometime, just for the heck of it, take your lover for a walk or for a nature ride along a bike trail. But before the actual walk or ride, go there beforehand and hide a gift somewhere along the trail for your lover.

The gift itself is completely up to you. It can be a bottle of their favorite perfume, a new piece of jewelry, etc. Have it gift wrapped with a card saying how much you are in love with them, so when the gift is discovered, they'll know you were the one that placed it there.

On the walk or ride, your lover may spot the hidden present and say, "Look! What's that?" and open the gift. Give your lover a chance to do just that, but if they fail to see it, then you will be the one to shout, "Hey, look what I've found!" Then hand the present and card over to your lover to unwrap.

However it happens, if your lover finds it or you have to, your mate will love the unique way you gave the gift and the thought behind it.

(72) The Treasure Hunt for Love

Dave and Beth had been together for some time and were truly, in love, but over a period of time, they began to take each others love for granted (as often happens in a relationship).

Both were romantics at heart, but with their busy work schedules, it sometimes became seemingly impossible to act on the romantic notions each had from time to time. Beth made a decision that it was time to act and ignite the flame of love which seemed to have dwindled to only a flicker.

Beth planned a treasure hunt for love and worked on all the details a week in advance so there would be no flaws in her plans. She planned it for the following Saturday, and knowing Dave's regular Saturday routine, here's what she did.

She told Dave she was getting up fairly early and would be spending her day shopping. She knew as soon as Dave was up and about he would get the morning paper from the porch and turn directly to the sports pages. Beth wrote the following note and placed it inside the paper's sports section as she left that morning.

Her note said, "Dearest Dave, you are undoubtedly the sexiest man I have ever seen. I light up when I'm near you and I want to be near you NOW! If you're interested in the most romantic time of your life, be sure and check the mail as soon as it's delivered."

She signed the note,"From your one true love and admirer in life."

This,of course, piqued Dave's interest and he could hardly wait for the mailman's delivery.

Beth had picked out a card and mailed it the day before, knowing it would arrive on Saturday with the local one-day mail service. She also recorded a message on a cassette tape and placed it in the tape player of Dave's car.

When the mail came, Dave rushed to the box, opened the card, and received the following message. "I love you and long to be with you. I want and need to be near you so much. If you think I would be worth the effort, take a short drive and listen to the tape in your car."

Again, it was signed, "From your one true love and admirer in life."

Dave immediately locked the house, started up the car, and turned the tape on. The tape first said, "Drive to the bookstore you always shop at, ask for Becky, identify yourself to her, and we're on our way." Then the song she had recorded for him began to play. It was the old Stevie Wonder classic, "YOU ARE THE SUNSHINE OF MY LIFE".

The Becky whom Dave asked for at the bookstore was a long-time friend of Beth's and was of course part of Beth's plan. Dave asked for her, identified himself as instructed, and Becky, who was expecting him, said, "Yes Dave, you have won a free gift and I'm supposed to give it to you."

She then presented Dave with a gift-wrapped book. Dave thanked her and as soon as he was back to the car he opened his package. It was a book entitled THE ART OF LOVE and

61

Beth had written the following note on the inside of the cover. "Although you need no coaching, spend the next hour reading over this book; you may find some interesting ideas you'll want to try. After reading for the next hour, await a phone call with further instructions." It was signed just as the other notes had been.

Dave did indeed read, but he found himself so anxious for his incoming phone call that he could hardly wait. In one hour, just as promised, the phone call came. A recording of another Stevie Wonder classic greeted him as the words and music proclaimed, "I JUST CALLED TO SAY I LOVE YOU". At the end of the song, a recorded message said, "If you wish to take advantage of that love, drive to the corner of Main and Broadway where you will see a phone booth. Go now, and answer that phone. It will ring in exactly 15 minutes."

Dave did as instructed by the recording. When he answered the call at the phone booth, an unfamiliar voice, which was that of another of Beth's friends, said, "Look directly across the street on the northwest corner and you will see a public mailbox. Taped to the bottom of the mailbox you will find a note with further instructions."

Dave went to the box, reached under and retrieved the card taped to the bottom, and read, "I'm so glad you've stuck with it this far. Now if you'll be standing in front of the coo-coo clock in your den at exactly four o'clock, you will begin to find out what this is all about." It was signed just as the other messages had been.

Four P.M. found Dave staring at the coo-coo clock on his den wall, and when the little birdie came out to do his thing, a small note was taped to its head. Dave grabbed at the note on the bird's second exit from the box, succeeded in pulling it free, and read the contents. "Play the tape in the glove compartment of your car."

Dave took off for the car once more, found the tape, put it in, and listened as it instructed him to shower, dress, and get ready for the most exciting night of his life. Then it said he would receive another call at 5:30 P.M.

Once bathed and dressed for his exciting evening, he paced the floor until the 5:30 call came with a recorded message to go to the Hyatt Regency Hotel and wait for a phone call at the pay phone closest to the west end of the lobby.

Once Dave arrived, he waited by the phone for close to five

minutes; then the call came and another unfamiliar voice said, "Go to the front desk, identify yourself, and they will have something for you."

He did so, and the lady gave him a small envelope. Dave found a note and key inside. The note said, "This is the key to a fantastic evening! Come to room 422 and use the key to unlock the door between you and all your fantasies."

When Dave used the key, he found a table set with a champagne dinner for two, complete with candelabra. Then Beth emerged from the adjoining bedroom looking as ravishingly beautiful as Dave could ever remember her and dressed even more sexy than he could have ever dreamed in his wildest fantasies.

The treasure hunt for love was over. Dave found his treasure, and Beth was true to her word; they had the most passionate night together ever. The flame of love was re-ignited in both their souls.

Beth had taken the initiative to follow up on one of her romantic notions and shown a little imagination, and she and Dave now have a love that's stronger than ever.

You too can do the same. You don't have to follow Beth's plan step by step. Use a little of your own imagination, put your own treasure hunt for love together, and marvel at the results.
It's fun, it's exciting, and it works!

(73) The Treasure Hunt (Part II)

Mark decided to take Marie on a second honeymoon for their upcoming wedding anniversary. That in itself was a romantic notion, but Mark thought about the whole idea and took it a few steps beyond.

He thought about the treasure hunt for love and made up his own little treasure hunt for Marie; here is what he did.

He went to a local mall and bought Marie a new set of luggage. Inside the small overnight bag of the set, he placed the following note, "Go to the Sears store in this mall and pick up a lay-a-way that's in your name."

He then left the luggage with the sales lady and asked her to make certain to tell Marie there was a note inside the baggage when she came to pick it up.

Mark then called Marie and told her she was to pick up a gift he had purchased for her at 11:00 A.M. and told her in what store she was to pick it up. That was the only phone call he made to her that day, and it was only placed to get her started on her hunt.

He had previously put four new outfits, new underwear, three pairs of shoes, and two sexy nightgowns in the lay-away. He did this so he could hide the items from Marie until the day of the hunt, and to make it part of the treasure she was hunting.

As soon as he made his call about picking up the luggage, he went to Sears, paid out the lay-away, placed a note inside one of the boxes telling Marie to go to another store in the mall where another package would be waiting for her to claim, and told the lady Marie would be picking up the lay-a-way some time before noon.

The note inside the lay-away box directed Marie to a cosmetic store in the mall where Mark had purchased a travel bag of cosmetics. It contained all the items Marie would need to take a short trip. Inside the bag was another note directing her to the next store, and just as before, Mark had paid for the gift in advance and asked the sales lady to tell Marie there was a note inside for her.

The note led Marie to a camera shop where he had purchased a new camera and plenty of film. Marie picked up the package and the salesman told her she was to meet her husband at the cocktail lounge at the local airport at 3:00 P.M.

64

When Marie arrived, she and Mark enjoyed a drink, then Mark presented her with two round-trip tickets to New Orleans, where they had gone on their first honeymoon.

Mark went to the car, packed into the new luggage the packages he had left at the various stores in the mall, and the two of them left for the second honeymoon.

Needless to say, the second honeymoon was something the two of them will never forget, but the treasure hunt leading up to it was something special as well, and Marie will treasure that thought almost as much as the trip itself.

You too can surprise your lover in such a fashion. You don't have to end up at the airport to take a trip. You can send them on a shopping spree treasure hunt where everything is prepaid and have them meet you for dinner as the last stop.

It's up to you where you want the hunt to end up, and what you want to purchase for them to pick up along the way. The bottom line is that the hunt is fun for them, and it is a romantic notion they will not soon forget.

(74) An Underwater Treasure Hunt

If you and your lover are into scuba or deep-sea diving, you can have an underwater treasure hunt on your next diving trip together by hiding a gift underwater for them.

Leave some signs leading your lover to the underwater treasure, and have sign attached to the gift itself that says, "This is for you Laura!"

You will have to set this up in advance by going to the diving site ahead of time and putting everything in place. When you do, make certain you attach a weight to the gift itself so it doesn't float away, and make sure the gift is something that the salt water won't ruin (like a bottle of their favorite perfume).

If you're not into diving, you can still use this idea in the backyard, or public pool.

You can leave a dozen roses tied to a weight at the bottom of the pool for them. Or, you can wrap a gift in wrapping paper, then dip it in hot wax to waterproof it, and weight it to the bottom of the pool for your lover to find.

It matters not which of these you do for your lover. They will find the idea both exciting and romantic of you.

(75) The Camping Trip With A Treasure Map

Alan decided to take Jean on a romantic camping trip. He wanted the trip to be special, so he planned it well in advance.
He went out two days before the big event and scouted around for the perfect location. He found an isolated island in the middle of a local lake which had a small natural beach area as well as good places to camp for a couple of nights.

Alan returned home to pack all the things he and Jean would need for a good time. While getting everything together, he thought how much fun it would add to the outing if he planned a treasure hunt for Jean as part of the festivities.

He went to a local jewelry store and purchased a nice necklace for her, had it gift wrapped, then placed it in a slightly larger box so he could bury it once they were on the island.

On the morning of the big event, Alan hitched up his boat and packed everything into the car. He and Jean put the boat into the lake and took off for their love island.

Alan thought of everything and the camp they set up had a tent for them to sleep in, lots of blankets in case the weather turned cool at night, a folding table and two chairs, tablecloths and candles for the table, camping torches to keep the bugs away, lanterns for extra light after dark, a tape player and tapes of soft music to enjoy, suntan oil for him to rub Jean with, plenty of grapes he could hand-feed her, an ice chest full of Jean's favorite food and drinks, camping tools, the gift he had brought to hide for her, and a bottle of champagne to celebrate with once she found the hidden treasure.

After lunch, while Jean was lying in the sun, Alan said he was going to take a walk around the island and would return shortly.

He took the box containing the gift to a wooded area on the island, buried it, and on his way back to the camp, he made a treasure map which would lead Jean to the hidden treasure.

Once he had returned, he wrote a note telling her there was a buried treasure on the island, attached the map to the note, and taped them to the handle of a small camping shovel next to the fire he had built earlier.

After dinner, while it was still light enough to go on the treasure hunt, Alan started to rebuild the dwindling fire. He asked Jean to hand him the shovel, and she, of course, found the attached note and map.

This got Jean excited to begin the hunt, and with shovel and map in hand, she immediately did so.

Alan followed close enough behind to make certain she read the map properly and stayed on the right trail to the buried treasure but he didn't join her in the hunt itself so Jean wouldn't be tempted to ask for verbal clues to assist her on her search.

Once she found the spot, she dug up her treasure, opened the outer box, then the gift-wrapped box, and was thrilled by the contents.

Needless to say, the necklace will always have a special meaning to Jean and the treasure hunt included in the camping trip was a romantic idea on Alan's part.

You too can plan such an outing. It doesn't have to be a camping trip; it can be a one-day outing if you prefer. You can plan-a picnic as opposed to a camping trip.

If you don't own a boat, you can borrow or rent one. One way or the other (two or three-day camping trip, or one-day) your lover is certain to enjoy the treasure hunt for their gift.

76) The Easter-Egg Hunt

Excite your lover by having an Easter-egg hunt with a grand prize at the end.

Get a package of the plastic eggs, write notes to put inside each egg, then hide the eggs wherever you wish. The first egg should be easily found and the note inside should give a good clue as to where the next egg is hidden.

The process continues until you have taken your lover over the entire area where the eggs have been hidden, and the last egg should have a note telling them where to go to claim the grand prize.

The grand prize is, of course, up to you. You can be waiting for them with a bottle of their favorite perfume, you can lead them to a place where you have left tickets to a ballgame or a play they have been wanting to see, or to a restaurant where you are waiting for them for a romantic dinner.

Again, the grand prize is completely up to you, and no matter the prize, they will have fun getting to it, and you should make the prize something you know they will enjoy.

(77) The Right Time

Anytime is the right time to give your lover a gift. One gift that's romantic and will always have a special meaning is an engraved watch.

Buy your lover a nice time piece and have it engraved on the back. Some inscriptions you can use are:

(1) "Without you, time stops!"
(2) "You're the only one I love to spend time with! "
(3) "My time is your time!"
(4) "There is no time without you!"
(5) "You're the time of my life!"
(6) "I love the time we spend together!"
(7) "The time I found you was the best time of my life!"
(8) "It's time you knew how I really feel about you!"
(9) "It's time to get married!"
(10) "It's time to say I love you!"
(11) "Time and time again, I love you!"

You may want to give the inscribed watch as an anniversary gift. If so, you can have it inscribed with, "Where has all the time gone? Happy anniversary!"

Any of these are special messages that your lover will cherish and the time piece itself will be secondary to the idea behind it as far as your lover is concerned.

A special gift that isn't very expensive or hard to make is a key chain tennis shoe with a candy kiss.

Most department stores have these small tennis shoe key chains, so they're rather easy to find. Take one of the miniature shoes, glue it to a piece of oak or cedar plank, (which you can get at a hardware store) spray it with a glossy finish, (so it will look good as well as keep) then place a candy kiss in the top of the shoe so it shows.

Make a small plaque that says, "I'd walk a mile for one of your kisses", and attach it to the plank, next to the small shoe.

You may choose to buy a pair of real tennis shoes, fill the shoes with a couple of bags of candy kisses, place some pink cotton in the bottom of the shoe box, and attach a note saying, "There is no limit to how far I'd walk for your kisses!" Then, gift wrap the box and have it delivered to your lover.

Either gift is romantic and should be delivered to your mate by special carrier. You can have the gift delivered to their place of work or to their home; it doesn't matter. What does matter is the fact that you sent the gift and they know you are always thinking of them and are truly in love.

A novel way to let your lover know exactly what's on your mind is to go to a novelty shop and purchase one of the rubber brains they have as gag-gifts.

Instead of giving it as a gag-gift, you make a nice plaque that can be hung on a wall and attach the rubber brain to the plaque. Have a small brass plate engraved with your message to your lover and attach it to the wooden plaque (just below where you have glued the rubber brain).

Some examples of the message you can have engraved are:

(A) "I have no mind without you!"
(B) "Where was my brain when I argued with you?"
(C) "In my mind, you're the only one for me!"
(D) "My mind agrees with what my heart already knew. I'm in love with you!"
(E) "I'd have to be out of my mind to ever leave you!"

You can also use this idea as a way of proposing marriage by having the engraving say, "My mind's made up! Let's get married!"

Once you have the rubber brain and brass engraved plate attached, gift wrap it and give it to your lover over a romantic dinner. They'll love it!

Take some empty Budweiser™ beer cans, a pair of tin-snips, a pair of needle-nose pliers, and you're on your way to making your lover a beautiful keepsake they will cherish forever.

To accomplish this feat, cut the Budweiser labels from the empty cans with the tin-snips, take the needle-nose pliers and shape the labels in the form of rose-petals, then put the petals together with Super-Glue to form them in the shape of a full rose.

Once you have made your first flower, take the tin-snips and cut a piece the entire length of the empty can. Roll the long piece with the pliers until it resembles a long stem for your rose. Attach the stem to the rose itself (with the Super-Glue) and you now have one long stemmed red rose.

You can stop with the single rose, or make a dozen if you would like. Some ideas for the completed gift are:

(A) Go to the hardware store and buy a small piece of wood to make a plaque with. Varnish the wood and have engraved, "This Bud's for you" across the bottom. Then glue the single rose above the engraving. Attach a hook on the back and it can be hung on the wall.

(B) Take an empty Bud can , glue it to the plaque, and place the long-stemmed rose in the pop-top opening. This can be set on a shelf, end table, night stand, or coffee table.

(C) If you've made a dozen of the roses, buy a nice vase, have "This Bud's for you" engraved on the vase, and place the dozen roses in it.

(D) You can also buy one of the water-filled, round, glass balls with the real single rose inside. Screw the bottom from the ball and remove the real rose. Replace the rose you remove with the rose you have made. Have a brass plaque or silver serving tray engraved with "This Bud's for you" and set the glass ball containing your rose on the tray or plaque. Again, this can be set on the coffee table, and it is sure to be a conversation piece.

Any of these ideas will mean a lot more to your lover than a gift you could go out and buy for them because you made it yourself, it was time consuming, and it shows how much you care.

On the next occasion that you are giving your lover a gift, a romantic way of presenting it is to attach the gift to a Teddy Bear (any size bear will do) with a card saying, "I LOVE YOU BEARY BEARY MUCH!"

If the gift is a necklace, you don't even have to wrap it; just place the necklace around the bear's neck, place the Teddy Bear in the seat of their car, on the bed, or some place they will easily discover it.

If you prefer gift-wrapping the present, tie a ribbon in your lover's favorite color around the bear's neck and attach the gift (such as a bottle of perfume) to the hanging ribbon.

For an added touch, you can tie the string of a helium filled balloon that says "I LOVE YOU" to the arm of the Teddy-Bear.

One thing is certain, your lover will enjoy the unique way you gave the gift.

(82) *Teddy In Bed*

Purchase a gold chain for your lover, then buy a large Teddy Bear and place the gold chain around the Teddy-Bear's neck.

Tie the string of a balloon around one arm of the Teddy-Bear and a nice card to the other arm. On the balloon, write, "I love you!" and on the card, say what you'd like, concerning the gift.

Lay the Teddy-Bear on the bed, spread the bear's arms open wide, (as if it wanted a big hug) and leave it for your lover to find.

Some ideas you can do, or write on the card are:

(A) Write, "I'd love to see you in this chain!" Or, "I love to see chains around you!"

(B) Write, "You look great in chains!"

(C) Write, "You're my Teddy-Bear!"

(D) Place a tape around the Teddy-Bear's arm with the old Elvis song "JUST WANNA BE YOUR TEDDY-BEAR" recorded on it.

(E) Put a teddy nightgown on the Teddy-Bear, and on the card write, "This teddy would look better on you!"

(83) *The Sweet Message*

Everyone has old cans, boxes, and maybe even an old heart-shaped candy box on a shelf somewhere collecting dust. Instead of sitting there as dust collectors, you can put them to good use to send a sweet message.

Fill the box with sugar, gift wrap it, and have it delivered by special carrier to your lover's work or home with a card attached. The card can say whatever you'd like, but of course your message must relate to the sugar in some way.

Some examples are:

(A) "I'm sweet on you!"

(B) "There is nothing as sweet as you!"

74

(C) "You are the sweetest thing in my life!"

(D) "The thoughts of you are so sweet to me!"

(E) "I miss your sugar!"

These are all sweet messages and it's the small act such as this that lets your lover know without a doubt that you do love them and think of them at all times.

84 The Sweet Messaage (Part Two)

Another way to send your lover a sweet message is to gift wrap a large jar of honey which you've had a small brass plaque made for and attached to the jar.

Some examples of the message you can have written on the plaque are:

(A) "I'm sweet on you!"

(B) "You are my sweetheart!"

(C) "You are sweeter than honey!"

(D) "You're the sweetest thing I've ever tasted!"

(E) "There's nothing as sweet as you!"

(F) "You are my honey!"

Have the gift-wrapped box containing your gift of honey delivered to your lover at work or at home. You can do this on a special day, such as a birthday, anniversary, etc., but it's best to send it on an ordinary day, and even better to send it on a day when you know things aren't going too well for your lover. It'll brighten the day and make things go a little better.

(85) I'm Nuts Over You

You can let your lover know just how you feel about them with this idea. Take your favorite eight-by-ten picture of your lover and place it in a nice frame. Glue sunflower-seeds all around the edges of the glass of the frame, then have a small brass plaque made with the message, "I'm nuts over you" printed on it.

Glue the brass plaque at the bottom of the glass cover of the frame, gift wrap the present, then give it to your lover over a romantic dinner.

(86) The Bunch Of Bananas

Take a pretty basket, fill it with a bunch of fresh bananas, cover it with plastic wrap, tie a red bow around the top, and have it delivered to your lover. With the basket, you can have a nice card with one of the following messages.

If you're trying to make up with your lover after an argument, say, "I miss you a whole bunch!" Or, "I'm going bananas because you are mad at me!"

If you are out of town and just want to let them know you're thinking of them, you can again say, "I miss you a whole bunch!" Or you can say, "I'm going bananas being away from you." You may want to combine the two by saying, "I'm going bananas because I miss you a whole bunch!"

If you want to send it just as a gift to say "I love you," you can write "I am bananas over you!" on the card.

These ideas are romantic ways to say "I'm sorry", I miss you", or "I love you". Try it next time you're out of town, have had a disagreement, or just want to say you care. See if it doesn't get the point across.

87 You're Number One

We all need to let our lover know they are the number one thing in our lives, and they need to hear it from us from time to time. A good way to say it is to buy a candle in the shape of the number ONE (like you often see on a birthday cake) and have it gift wrapped and delivered to your lover. Along with the candle, have a card attached which says:

(A) "You're the number ONE thing in my life!"
(B) "You'll always be number ONE with me!"
(C) "You are the only ONE for me!"
(D) "I'm so glad I found the ONE and only you!"

Again, you can make use of this idea to propose marriage by saying on the card, "You are the ONE I want to marry! Will you marry me?"

88 Swept Away

Go to a novelty shop that has the decorative brooms that hang on the wall and buy one for your lover. Have a brass plaque made and attached that says, "You swept me off my feet! Love, Bill."

Gift wrap it and present it to your lover after a romantic dinner. It's a gift which they can hang on the wall and forever cherish.

89 I'm Stuck On You

This is a simple little thing to do for you lover, but one that's certainly romantic and will be meaningful to them as well.

Go to a local florist and purchase a potted cactus. Have it decorated with red ribbon around it and attach a nice card which says, "I'm stuck on you!" Have the cactus delivered to their home or at work.

If you'd prefer to present the gift yourself instead of having it delivered, you can make a small sign that says, "I'm stuck on you!" and stick it in the planter the cactus is in; then, present the cactus to your lover after a romantic dinner together.

One way or the other, your lover will be pleased!

90 The Spice Of Life

Take a large spice jar, one at least six inches tall, and empty the contents. Take a picture of your lover, place it inside the empty jar, then fill the jar with the potpourri you have emptied.

Place the corrugated lid (the one with the small holes) back on the jar so the smell will filter through.

On the outside of the jar, just above the picture of your lover, make a tag to write on, or have a small brass plaque made, and glue it on the jar. On the hand-made tag or brass plaque, have engraved the word "You are the spice of my life!"

You can gift wrap it with pretty paper and bow to give as a gift. You can buy an L-shaped plaque which will hang on the wall with the jar sitting on it and give that as a gift; or, you can keep it stored away until the next time your lover has a bad day, (for whatever reason) then present them with your gift. It's sure to make the day go better.

91 You Mean The World To Me

Here is an idea you can use to let your lover know that they do indeed mean the world to you.

Buy a world globe, have it gift wrapped and delivered to your lover. With the gift-wrapped box containing the globe, have a nice card which says something like:

(A) "You mean the world to me!"
(B) "I have the whole world because I have you!"
(C) "There is no one in the world as wonderful as you!"
(D) "There is nothing in the world I wouldn't do for you!"
(E) "Without you, my world would be empty!"
(F) "In this whole world, you're the only one for me!"

You can even use this idea to propose marriage by writing on the card, "There is no one in the world I would rather be with! Will you marry me?"

92 A Self-Made Valentine's Day Card

Instead of going out and buying a ready-made Valentine's Day card, be a little more personal by giving your lover a homemade card. It will mean more to them!

To accomplish this, buy a piece of red poster board, fold it in half, write a romantic message from you to your lover inside, and even glue in a recent picture if you would like.

Go through every pocket of all your clothes, each drawer in the house, the glove compartment of your car, boxes in the closets, places you stash away junk---anyplace where you might find mementos from your times together. Look for old movie stubs, ballgame ticket rain-checks, matchbook covers, an old note they wrote you, a swizzle stick from a restaurant where the two of you go, the page from a calendar that shows your anniversary, a lock of your hair, anything personal.

Once you have them all together, glue them to the front of the card in a collage which is of your own design and pleasing to look at.

It makes a perfect Valentine's Day card that your lover will cherish forever.

CHAPTER THREE
MAKING UP

No one agrees on everything, and no matter how much you are in love, you are going to have disagreements with your lover. At times, the simple disagreement can turn into an out and out quarrel, and when it does, (if you're truly in love) you're soon over it and want to make up with your mate. That's what this chapter deals with - ways to do just that, ways to make up with your lover and put the relationship back on firm ground.

93 The Broken Heart

A fantastic idea for making up with your lover after an argument is the flower arrangement of the broken heart.

Order a heart-shaped arrangement of red carnations with white carnations down the middle, indicating a crack in the heart. You may also have one half red and the other all white, still denoting a broken heart. With the arrangement comes the simple message, (on a beautiful card) "I'm heart broken."

Have them delivered to their place of work or the home, whichever you prefer, then sit back and wait for the return message; it should be a positive one.

94 A Broken Heart

If you and your lover are having a disagreement over something, and you wish to make up with them, call them up and say you really need to talk. Invite them over for dinner and conversation.

Once they accept the invitation, get a solid red tablecloth, cut it out in the shape of a heart, sew the edge of it so it won't unravel, then cut it down the center, or paint a white crack down the center to represent your broken heart.

Place the tablecloth on the dinner table and have a candlelight dinner for the two of you. Over dinner, tell your lover how heartbroken you are over the fight, and ask if they will please forgive you.

The odds are that your lover will appreciate the sincere apology as well as the symbolic gesture of the broken-hearted tablecloth, and will forgive you. They'll probably want the tablecloth as a keepsake.

If you have the wood-working skills, you can make a dinner table in the shape of a heart, paint it red, then paint a white crack down the middle of it. If you don't have the skill to make one yourself, you can hire it done for you, then do the same as you would have done with the tablecloth.

You can also use this idea to propose marriage by painting the message, "Will you marry me?" on the tablecloth, or table, instead of painting or cutting the crack for the broken heart.

Invite your lover over for a romantic dinner with the candlelight, soft music, and their favorite foods. When she sits down for dinner, your proposal of marriage is right in front of her to see in big, bold letters.

(95) The Painted Box

An empty box can be used as a tool for making up with your lover too. To use the empty box for this purpose, paint the inside of the box black, then tape a note to the bottom of the inside saying, "My life is empty without you!" Or, "The future looks so black without you in my life!"

Once you have the inside painted black and the note inside, gift wrap the box and have it delivered to your lover. If you want, you can add something as a weight so the box feels as if there is something inside.

(96) Picture Pieces

This idea is good to help you make up with your lover. Take a picture of yourself, cut it up into several pieces like the pieces of a puzzle, put the pieces inside an envelope with a note, and mail it to them special delivery.

The note can say, "You're the only one who can put the pieces of my life back together again," or, "I'm falling apart without you in my life."

You can say, "Without you, I'm falling to pieces", or you may prefer to cut a picture of the two of you together into pieces and mail it with a note saying, "I'm all broken up about us. Please give me some help in putting us back together".

If you desire, before cutting the picture into pieces, you can write a message on the back of the picture saying how much you really love them. When they have put the picture together, the message is then clear for them to read.

(97) Puzzled Love

It's not wise to be a puzzle to the man or woman of your dreams! In a strong relationship, both partners should pretty well know the other's thoughts and desires.

Though this is true, you can use a puzzle to make up after an argument, to ask for their hand in marriage, or to just have some fun with as a gift.

To do this, you can buy a puzzle with a nice scene, or take a photo of yourself to a photo specialty shop and have them make a puzzle from your photo. This service is available in most places, but if it's not in your city, it is available by mail.

Put the puzzle together, write a message on the back, then take it apart and give it to your lover.

To use the puzzle to make up after a disagreement, you can write something like, "You're the only one who can put my life back together again!"

To just give it as a gift, you can write, "My life was in pieces before you put it together for me", or a simple "I love you, or anything you desire to write.

You may choose to have the puzzle made from a photo of you in a sexy outfit with a personal message on the back saying how much you desire to be in your lover's arms.

You can propose marriage by puzzle by writing, "Will you marry me?" on the back, or, have your picture taken holding a sign asking them to marry you, then have the puzzle made from that photo.

You can use the puzzle to send any message you wish.

98) The Heart-Shaped Box

The heart shaped candy box you usually associate with Valentines Day can be used on many other occasions and for various reasons.

You can use one to make up with your lover after a disagreement, to make a marriage proposal, or just to send as a special gift.

If you want to use one to help break the ice after an argument, empty the candy, write a personal message in the bottom of the box, then replace the candy. Once your lover has removed a few pieces of the candy, they will see the writing, remove the candy, and read your message saying how sorry you are the two of you had an argument.

If you want to use one to propose marriage, remove the candy, tape a left-hand glove to the bottom of the box, place an engagement ring on the ring finger of the glove, and write the message, "Will you marry me?" below the glove.

To send or give the box as a special gift, again remove the candy, place the box over a picture of yourself, trace around the heart shape of the box, cut the picture to fit inside the heart, glue or tape the picture inside, replace the candy, then put a small hook on the back of the box so that when the candy is all eaten, the heart can be hung on the wall with your picture inside.

Another way to use the heart~shaped box as a tool for helping you make up after an argument is to use the box only, (without the candy).

To accomplish this, empty the candy and place a nice card inside saying, "My heart is empty without you!"

You can use the heart shaped box to send any message you wish, with or without the candy, and the shape of the box makes it romantic within itself. So save the boxes after Valentines Day and put them to use the year round.

⟨99⟩ Boxes

Boxes can be put to romantic uses in several different ways. Say you've had a disagreement with your lover; you can use an empty box to help ease the tensions between you.

To do this, take an empty box and place the following note inside: "My life is empty without you!" Then gift wrap the box complete with ribbons and bow, place a single rose under the ribbon, and have the package delivered to your lover. It will help because they will know you do care and are hurting inside because of the argument.

You can also use the boxes to propose marriage. To do this, take a small ring box with an engagement ring inside, put in a note asking if they will marry you, place the ring box in a slightly larger box, then that box in an even larger one. Repeat this process box after box until you finally have one large package with all the smaller boxes inside.

Gift wrap the large box and have it delivered to your lover. It will look as if they have a huge present to open. Once they get into the first box, they will continue to open box after box until they find the note and ring. It's romantic and your lover will be certain to find the ring worth all the trouble of searching the boxes for it.

You don't have to have a special occasion to use this idea. You can wrap a small gift in a small box and use the box-after-box method just for the fun of it to give your lover a gift from out of the blue. They will love the novel way you presented the gift to them.

100 The Black Book

You can use construction paper to make a book for your lover if the two of you have had a disagreement and you wish to tell them how sorry you are the two of you are having a problem.

Take black construction paper, fold it in half, (about five pieces should be about right) staple the center of the folded pages to put it in a book form, then take a white crayon to number the pages on the corner of each page.

The last page will be the only one with any writing on it. On the last page, again in white crayon, write, "There is no sunshine in my life without you!" Or, "The pages of my life are black without you!"

Send the book to your lover by special delivery and once they have received it, they'll know your feelings.

(101) The Three Part Message

This idea is to be used as a tool for making up after a disagreement with the love of your life.

There are variations in the plot itself and you can use your own judgement as to what alterations to make to fit your own particular needs.

The main concept is that the message comes in three parts and is delivered with flowers. You can send a message a day, or one an hour if you prefer, but be sure to use your partner's favorite flower.

When sending the flowers, again, you have several choices. You can send a solitary flower, or a dozen if you would like. Since the message comes in three parts, you may choose to send the first note with a single flower, the second with a half dozen, and the third with a dozen of their favorites.

Note one comes with the words, "If you still love me", or, "If you will forgive me." Note two says, "Tie a yellow ribbon around", and three tells them where to tie the ribbon.

It can be anywhere you desire. You can go along with the lines of the old song and use, "The old Oak tree" if you happen to have one in your yard; if not, you can say "the mailbox", "the lightpole", or anything around that would be convenient and conspicuous.

(102) *Write It Down*

When we have a disagreement with our lover, the disagreement can sometimes turn into an out and out argument. When this happens, we often end up saying things we don't really mean and we always regret saying them.

The same is true to a certain extent when we try making up. We want to say all the right things, let our mate know we do love them, and just how much they mean to us; but, no matter how much we rehearse the words, it never seems to come out just as we planned.

A good way to prevent this is to sit down and write out just exactly what you want to say. Write a letter saying why you think the two of you had the argument to begin with, how stupid it was to let the disagreement get out of hand, how sorry you are and how much you love them. Then, give them all the reasons why you do.

Once you have your letter completed, don't rehearse and try to commit it to memory. In your passion of trying to deliver your message and conveying your feelings, you will always leave something out you truly want to say, or, worse yet, say something the wrong way and make things worse.

This being the case, (most of the time) tell your lover you have something to say, sit them down, then read your letter word for word. This way, you leave nothing to chance, you free yourself of the burden of saying the wrong thing, and last—but not least, you're not dependent on a memory which has been impaired by your emotions over the argument.

If we could all say just the right things, arguments would be few and far between. Our chances of saying the intended are certainly greater if we write them out as opposed to speaking extemporaneously.

CHAPTER FOUR
ADVERTISING

Advertising the fact that you're in love, want to get married, or would like to go out with someone, is a romantic way of proclaiming your intentions. This chapter gives you several ideas on how to go about advertising just what you have on your mind. These ideas are sure to let them know that they do indeed occupy the number one spot in your heart.

To send a message with signs, you can make some heart-shaped signs from plywood, or take ready-made signs (such as for sale signs) and cut them into a heart shape. Then cover the signs with red paper, or paint them red.

Once you have enough signs to give your lover the intended message, paint the letters on with white paint, space the signs out at a distance of about one hundred feet along the route your lover drives when returning from work, shopping, etc.

You can put one word on each sign to say something like, "I love you Alice, more than you'll ever know, from Dan." This message would take one dozen signs, so if you don't have enough signs for this, you may choose to write two or three words on each as opposed to the single word signs.

You can use this idea to say anything you would like, such as, "Will you marry me Jan? From Darryl." "Happy anniversary Lisa, from Don." Or, "Happy Valentine's Day Linda, from Lloyd."

You can use this idea to convey the message that you are sorry for an argument by cutting one of the heart-shaped plywood signs in half, putting each half on a stake, and placing them side by side in the ground at the intersection next to your lover's house, or in their front yard. On the two halves, you put the words, "I'm heart broken!"

Instead of the heart-shaped sign, you can make one in the shape of a birthday cake, complete with candles, and write, "Happy Birthday Debbie, from Jason."

You can announce the arrival of a new baby by making a sign in the shape of a Stork with diaper and baby clutched in its beak, with the words painted on it, "It's a boy!" Or, "It's a girl!"

Most local airports have a company which advertises by flying banners. Through such companies you can hire a small plane to fly over a designated area pulling a large banner with a personalized message.

If you have a question, statement, or combination of the two, you can certainly ask or say what's on your mind to the receiver in person, but a very romantic way to get the message across is through these flying banners, and it will be a memory that will last a lifetime.

If your city or town doesn't have one of these services, you can rent billboard space beside a road your lover travels daily, rent advertising space on the local baseball field's outfield fence, or have your message flashed on the ball-field scoreboard.

Take your lover on a picnic and have the plane fly over with the message, or have it fly over the beach while the two of you are out taking in some sun.

If you have rented billboard space by the road, they will of course see and read your message as they drive by.

If you have rented the outfield sign or scoreboard message service, take them to a ball game. You can even have the ball game announcer announce your message over the P.A. system if you'd like.

The message can be whatever you would like for the occasion, such as, (I) "Linda, will you marry me? From Alan." (2) "I love you Beth! From Jack." (3) "Can we go out some time soon Mary? From Bill."

You can send the message "Happy Anniversary","Happy Birthday", etc. Whatever your reason, no matter the statement or question, this is a romantic way of getting the point across.

(105) Commercial Love

See someone in the sales department of one of your local radio or television stations to discuss the cost of running your own commercial on the air. Have your commercial written out for them in advance. They will time the ad, edit it to fit into the time slot you want, (thirty or sixty seconds) then set up the studio time for you to come in and do the taping.

Once you have cut your tape and paid for the ad to run, they will give you a print-out of available times your ad can be seen (if you have chosen T.V.) or heard (if you have picked radio).

Once you have checked off the times your ad is to run, make certain your lover is tuned in to the station carrying your ad at those times.

Your ad can be for any number of reasons. You can propose marriage, ask someone you've recently met out for a first date, recite a list of all the reasons you are in love with them, tell them "Happy birthday", "Happy anniversary", or just say, "I love you!"-

You can make the commercial humorous if you'd like by talking about something the two of you did in the past that always provokes laughter when the two of you think back on it.

If you would like, you can take the idea one step further. If you have some old slides of the two of you, you can go to a local movie theater, tell the manager what you would like to do, give him the slides, and at that night's movie, he can flash them on the screen with the message, "Happy Anniversary Becky, from Don."

If you have some old home movies, you can have the manager show them and then give your message of love. Take your mate to the movie that night and see the surprise on their face when the personal slides or home movies begin to show on the screen.

(106) Bus Advertisements

Advertisements on the side or rear of city buses are a rather inexpensive way to advertise, and thousands of people see them everyday.

Renting available sign space on your city's buses is an outstanding way to give your lover a message. You can propose marriage by having the sign say, "Will you marry me Debbie J.? From Jerry H."

You can just say, "I love you Mike, from Mary," or put any personal message you'd like from you to your lover.

It doesn't cost that much, and so many people will see it. But most important, your lover will see it on the bus that passes their home or work place, as well as on the buses they see as they drive around town, and they'll love it!

(107) *Radio Messages*

Most radio stations are rather easy to work with when you have a message for someone or a song dedication.

This being the case, call up the D.J. at the station who is on the air when your lover usually tunes in and ask them to dedicate a particular love song to your mate. After the D.J. has done so, he can read a message to your lover which has been prepared by you.

Some examples of the message you can write out for the D.J. to read are:

(A) "We interrupt this program to announce that John Smith would like to know if Mary Jones would marry him."

(B) "We interrupt this program to announce that Sam Jones would like to know if Susie Smith would go to dinner with him tonight."

You can use the radio message for a number of reasons. Not only is it a romantic way to propose marriage or ask that special someone out on a first date, but you can also just say, "Happy Birthday", Happy Anniversary, or, a simple "I love you!"

Once you have the plan set in motion and the D.J. is ready to dedicate the song and give your message, make certain the person to receive the message is tuned in.

Once the song and message have been aired, you can call up that special person in your life and get their response. It should be a positive one.

For a very small amount of money, you can place an advertisement in your local paper saying, "Happy Birthday", "Happy Anniversary", "Will you marry me?", or any message you desire to send.

You can place an ad to make up with your lover by saying, "One broken heart wanting desperately to return home!"

For slightly more money you can run a box ad, which is a little larger, and again, you can use the paper to give your lover any message you desire.

You may have to drop a few subtle hints to your lover about the ad to make certain they read it, or just come right out and tell them to do so, but once they see your advertisement, they'll know you do love them and are always thinking of them.

CHAPTER FIVE
TRIPS

Taking a trip, be it on business or for pleasure, always takes some pre-planning. This chapter focuses on both types of trips with the intent of giving you a few romantic ideas to add to your plans to help make any trip you take a fanciful happening and wonderful experience for both you and your mate.

An Out-Of-Town Surprise

The next time your mate has to go out of town on a business trip, and you know in advance where they are staying, call the manager of the hotel and tell them what you intend to do.

Find out what flight your mate is to be on, then make reservations for yourself on the next flight.

Take your lover to the airport, kiss them good-bye, and say how much you're going to miss them. See them to the plane, then just kill time until your plane departs.

When you arrive in the city just behind your lover, take a cab to the hotel, tell the manager you have arrived, and have them let you into your lover's room.

When your lover comes in from his or her business meeting, have the room ready for a romantic dinner with candlelight, champagne, etc.

If you run into a stubborn hotel manager who refuses to grant you entrance, tell one of your mate's co-workers who's on the trip what you have in mind. Have them ask your mate to meet them in the hotel dining room for dinner at a certain time. When your mate enters the dining room, you'll be there in place of the co-worker and you can have the table there set for the romantic dinner.

One way or the other, it'll be a surprise to your lover and the two of you can enjoy the out-of-town trip together.

(110) A Mountain Getaway

You can use this idea on a birthday, anniversary, or just for the fun of it. Whatever the occasion, you and your lover are sure to enjoy the time together.

Rent a mountain chalet overlooking a lake or some similar nice romantic view, (a snow-covered mountain peak is nice).

Make sure the cabin has no phone, T.V., or any other outside interferences. Have a big fire built in the fireplace for the two of you to lie in front of and enjoy. Have all the food and drinks you'll need to last throughout your stay, and just enjoy the romance the seclusion is certain to bring on.

If you're there at the time of year that snow may be falling, it would be nice to rent a chalet with an outside hot-tub so you and your lover can enjoy the warm water while the snow falls around you.

(111) Pack Their Bags

If your lover must travel frequently on their job, next trip, pack their bags for them. Inside the suitcase, place a special gift from you in a gift-wrapped box. Along with the gift, put dated love letters with instructions that they are not to open each letter until the date on the envelope.

Each letter should state how much you love and miss them, how you can't wait for their return, and count down the days, such as, "Three more days until I'm in your arms once again", "Two more days until I'll be lying beside you in our own bed", "One more day until I can kiss you once again".

The gift can be something nice you have picked out for them, or something you've had made for them, like a picture of you in a sexy nightgown, which they can set beside the bed.

If you prefer, the gift can be something sexy for yourself to wear with a card saying, "When you return home, I'll model this for you!"

Regardless of the gift, your lover will appreciate your thoughtfulness, the love letters, and will be that much more anxious to return home to you.

(112) Brighten up their Trip

The next time your lover has to take a trip out of town, call the hotel where they are to be lodging ahead of time and have them put a gift-wrapped present from you on the bed where they will find it upon arrival. Have a nice card from you with the gift saying, "Hope this little gift helps to brighten up your trip."

If you are to be out of town for a few days you can use the same idea in reverse by having a gift special delivered back to your mate at home with a card saying, "Just wanted you to know that I love and miss you."

This will let them know for certain that they are always on your mind.

(113) A Barefoot Cruise

For a special romantic vacation together, plan a barefoot cruise for you and your lover without their knowledge of it.

There are several places along the coast that offer these cruises and they are truly romantic. Surprise your lover with one!

The romantic things you can do on a barefoot cruise are limitless. At each port of call, you and your lover can take moonlight strolls barefooted along the beach.

For a special keepsake from the barefoot cruise, write in the sand the message, "I love you (your lover's name) so much!" Take a picture of your love letter in the sand, and mail it home. When you return home, it will be waiting in the mail box for your lover to enjoy.

If you don't have the time for a complete barefoot cruise vacation, you might try an overnight cruise, or a cruise of only a few hours. Such cruises are also available and enjoyable.

Tell your lover you need a short vacation. Take a few days off from work, or just make plans for a weekend, then make it the greatest short vacation your mate could ever imagine.

Have a limousine pick the two of you up the morning you depart, take you to a nice hotel right in your hometown, (where you have the honeymoon suite reserved) and when you enter the room, carry your lover over the threshold, have flowers, a fruit basket, chilled champagne, and brunch awaiting.

The entire stay, you should have all your food and drinks served to you by room service. You should also have a nice gift to present your lover upon arrival, and another to present just before departing the hotel for home.

All of these arrangements will have to be taken care of by you in advance of your arrival, so make a check list of the things you want done to make the short stay the most memorable vacation you and your lover have ever had together.

If you are married, a short stay like this is a perfect way to spend an anniversary weekend.

(115) *Queen for a Day*

Put this plan into action on an ordinary Friday afternoon. When it's not a birthday, anniversary, or any other special day, pack your lover a bag with the things she'll need for a weekend trip, put the bags in the trunk of the car without her knowing anything about the bags or your plans, then tell her you are going to cook her favorite dinner for her.

The two of you go to the supermarket and let her pick out everything she wants for that dinner. When you return home, draw a warm bath for her to enjoy while you prepare the food. Have the table set fit for a queen, with flowers, your finest china, and silverware, then have the dinner by candlelight.

After you have enjoyed the dinner, let her relax while you wash dishes and clean up. Once everything is cleaned and put away, tell her you want to take a drive in the country, but instead of the country drive, head to an out-of-town hotel where you have the Honeymoon suite reserved for the weekend, carry her across the threshold, and enjoy the weekend together as if it was a second honeymoon.

⟨116⟩ *The Continuous Letter*

This idea is good if you are going to be out of town for a few days and want to send your mate a romantic letter. It is also a good way to ask that person you only recently met out on a first date.

If you're sending your lover a message from out of town, write a letter saying how you feel, and how you wish the two of you were together. Then, depending on how many days you are to be gone, or how many notes you wish to send, break the letter up into several small notes.

To do this, fold the completed letter in half, draw several hearts on the folded letter, and cut them out. Now you have a letter with several heart-shaped openings in the paper which there is no way your partner can read until you send the heart-shaped pieces you have cut from the page itself.

On the first day, you mail the letter (minus the cut-out hearts), on the second day, you mail the first heart, the third day, mail the second heart, and so on.

As your lover receives each missing heart, they will place them in the opening in the page, and after receiving the last missing piece, the continuous letter is complete; they now have your love letter in full and can work the puzzle.

The last part of the continuous letter should ask them to meet you for dinner on the night you are to return, and should tell them where to meet you for the romantic dinner.

To use this idea for asking that special someone out on a first date, write a letter saying how attracted you are to them, how wonderful they seem to be, how you would like to get to know them better, then ask them to dinner and tell them where to meet you for the romantic meeting.

In both cases, whether you are sending your message to your mate from out of town, or sending the letter to ask someone out for the first time, you should send a flower (or flowers) with each part of the note.

If you send a single flower with each section of the note, you may wish to send a different type of flower with each. If not, you can send a single rose with each. Either way, it's a romantic way to send your message and you can expect positive results.

The next time you and your lover are taking a trip together, write them a letter saying how much you enjoyed the trip, how great it was being together, then add a few things to the letter that you anticipate, or know in advance, will happen on the trip.

You can say how wonderful it was being together at a particular restaurant, (where you know for certain the two of you will be dining) how sexy they looked each night, and cover other details of the trip that you feel fairly certain will take place.

Close the letter with the lines, "The reason I could predict such a great time and send this letter in advance is I knew I would have a wonderful trip because you were with me!"

Date the letter on the day you are to depart and mail it to your lover's home address so it will be waiting in the mail when the two of you return home.

Your mate will enjoy the novelty of a pre-dated letter and your feelings that you always have a wonderful time with them present.

If you are to be out of town for a few days, you can let your lover know how much you'll be missing them by writing little love notes and dating them for each day you will be away.

Date the first note for the first day you'll be gone and write how much you hated to leave them behind, how you'll miss them, and how you hope they'll miss you as well.

The second day's note should be similar to the first and can say how much you truly love them.

The third day can say how you hope they are enjoying themselves and you can't wait to return and enjoy each other's company.

However many days you will be gone, there should be a note with that day's date on the envelope, and you should give your lover instructions to open each note on the day marked.

The last day's note will say how glad you are the day has come that you will be back together, and what time you will be back. Also tell them to be ready for a romantic dinner at whatever time you will be back.

⟨119⟩ *Puzzle Postcards*

If you're going to be out of town for a few days, get ten postcards, and in big letters, write a message to your lover saying how much you love and miss them. Then shuffle the postcards up so they are no longer in order and the message cannot be read until put back in proper order.

Mail the postcards to your lover. You can mail them two at a time or all at once if you'd like. The thing is, you've made a puzzle out of your postcard message. Your lover will solve the puzzle, read your message of love, and enjoy the unique way you sent it.

⟨120⟩ *A Letter About Your Mystic Lover*

When you and your lover return from a trip, write a letter about the trip, what a great time you had, how you hated to see the trip come to an end, and how sexy and lovely your lover was.

Instead of saying "you", or calling your lover by name in the letter, make your mate out to be a mysterious person by saying the woman, or man, whichever the case may be, was what made the stay away from home so special and exciting.

In the entire letter, refer to your mate as the man or woman "I was with" and it will make the letter more romantic as you talk about your mystic lover.

The letter should be exclusively about your mate, but written as if you were speaking about someone you had never met before, or had ever seen since.

Once completed, hide the letter in a spot where your lover will easily find it. When they do find it, and read about the wonderful times the two of you had, (in the romantic style of writing you have used,) romantic feelings will flow over them once again.

If your job requires that you travel and be out of town on occasion, next time try this idea to let your lover know you're thinking of them.

Call up an establishment that delivers prepared meals and order your lover's favorite breakfast delivered to their home. Tell them at what time you'd like it delivered, then at that time, call up your lover long distance and say, "I was just thinking about you and decided I'd like to have breakfast with you this morning".

The two of you can chat over the phone while you enjoy your long distance breakfast. The idea will thrill your lover to think you care so much about them.

The next time you and your lover must be out of town for a few days, and you happen to be staying at a hotel where you must ride an elevator, you can impress your mate with this idea.

Once you have checked in and know what floor you are to be on, make dinner reservations. Then, talk to the service personnel on each floor to put your plan in motion.

Go out and purchase the items you'll need and give one item to each employee you have secured for the plan. For a nice tip, they will be waiting on each floor to present a gift to your mate as the elevator stops at each floor.

You let the service people know the exact time you will be returning from dinner, and once you and your lover are in the elevator, you punch the buttons for every floor between the lobby and the floor your room is on.

As the elevator door opens on floor one, someone will be waiting with a lovely card from you saying how lucky you are to be there with your lover and how much you have been looking forward to this trip. On floor two, someone will present you a dozen roses, which you will then give your mate. On floor three, someone will be waiting with a bottle of chilled champagne and two glasses. On floor four, someone will give you a nice gift-wrapped box, and inside it will be a sexy nightgown.

Once you reach your floor, someone will be waiting by the elevator to escort you to your door, open it for you, pour your champagne, and a warm bath and spread rose petals leading to the bath.

The number of gifts depends on the number of stops you must make between the lobby and your floor, and the gifts can be anything you desire to give.

You can even use this idea as a way to propose marriage by having one of the gifts presented be an engagement ring and the card waiting on floor one can ask your mate to marry you.

For whatever reason you employ this idea, it's sure to be an impressive ride up for your lover.

(123) Just a Little Peek

The next time your husband or boyfriend is to be out of town for a few days and you're to pick him up at the airport, train station, etcetera, dress for the occasion!

Set this up by having a single rose with pink ribbon delivered to his hotel room the day before he is due back. With the rose, send a nice card saying you have a big surprise in store for him when he returns.

When the hour arrives, wear a long coat, high heels, and a see-through nightie. As soon as he arrives, and when no one is looking, FLASH HIM!

If you're really daring, you may choose to wear nothing at all under the coat.

This is certain to excite your lover and make him happier than ever to be returning home to you!

(124) Unique Arrival

If you are to be out of town for a few days, send your lover a gift each day you are gone. For instance, if you are to be gone four days, on day on, a small package should be delivered to your lover (containing a small gift such as a piece of jewelry).

On day two, a slightly larger package should arrive with something like a new dress enclosed. The third day, an even larger box should be delivered with a suitable gift enclosed.

On the fourth day (which is the day you are to return) make arrangements with a couple of friends in advance, and when you return, get inside a large box, have them gift wrap it, then deliver (to your lover) the large box with you inside.

When they open the box, you will emerge with a bottle of champagne with two glasses and the two of you can enjoy your return.

Your lover will never forget any of the gifts, and your unique arrival will be the most special gift they could have ever received.

CHAPTER SIX
FOOD

Romance and food seem to go together like hand and glove. Conjure up practically any romantic notion, and chances are, food is involved in some respect. Be it a romantic candlelight dinner, a picnic outing, a cook-out on the beach, a back-yard barbecue, etc. and the setting for a romantic evening is there as a natural result. What you do with the romantic opportunity is completely up to you, so this chapter shares many ideas on food and romance to help you make the evening of the occasion one that will not soon be forgotten.

(125) A Horse and Carriage Picnic

Go out in the country some place where you can rent a horse and carriage for the afternoon. Have a picnic basket full of your lover's favorite food and drink packed. Load the basket in the carriage and take off through the country-side.

Once you find a suitable spot, enjoy the picnic lunch. Spend some time talking about how wonderful it is for the two of you to spend time alone together, then spend the rest of the afternoon riding through the country-side the old fashioned way.

It's sure to be an afternoon both you and your lover will enjoy, probably so much so that you'll want to repeat it often.

(126) Food Messages

You can have fun with food by using it to send little messages to your lover. The most common way, and the way we've all seen, is the written message on a cake.

We've all had cakes with "Happy birthday" written on them, but you don't have to limit this old standard to birthdays, anniversaries, etc. You can use it to say anything you desire. You can give your mate a cake on an ordinary day that just says "I love you" written across it. You can have "Will you marry me" on it to propose marriage, or, as I said, anything you may wish to say romantic to your lover.

There are other ways to give your lover a message with food, and you don't have to write anything. You can fix pancakes, eggs, meat loaf, sandwiches, or cookies, cut them in the shape of a heart, and serve them to your lover. They will get the message!

You can use the cookies as a way of making up with your

mate after an argument. To do this, bake a large cookie in the shape of a heart, break it in half, (or make what looks like a crack through it with sugar or frosting) and give them the message you're heart broken.

You can go all out if you'd like and serve your lover a special candlelight dinner with all the food in the shape of hearts. The first item served can be a tossed salad with little carrot slices spelling out "I love you" on top, and the dessert can be a cake with "Will you marry me?" printed across it.

(127) The Perfect Picnic

Pick a day out that you know in advance will be a free day for you and your lover, then plan the perfect picnic for the two of you. A couple of days before your planned outing, scout around and find the perfect spot for the big event and make it a picnic your lover will never forget.

To accomplish this, have a limousine arrive at the designated time the two of you plan to depart, but don't tell your love the mode of transportation in advance. The limo should be the first surprise of the day.

Have the chauffeur drive to the place you have chosen, where, with luck, there is a stream, lake, creek, or some body of water. He will then open the doors for the two of you, spread a tablecloth on the ground, or open up a fold-out table and two chairs, light candles, pour wine, (grape juice will be great if you prefer non-alcoholic drinks), and serve the food from the picnic basket.

You should then collect some wild flowers which are around, put them in a vase you have packed, and place them in the center of the table or tablecloth on the ground.

Have the driver collect some fire wood and build a fire. Once he has finished the chore, he should drive off a short distance so you and your lover are left alone. He will be out of sight so the two of you have some privacy, but will be close enough by so you can call him with a toot of an air horn. You can blow the horn for him if you need him to rebuild the fire when it begins to dwindle, pour more wine, or just wait on the two of you in general.

After the two of you have enjoyed your lover's favorite foods, lie back and listen to some soft romantic music on the tape player, and feed your lover grapes as they enjoy another glass of wine or grape juice.

Once the picnic is over and you're ready to depart, have the limo return, and while the driver is cleaning up, packing the picnic supplies, and so on, you can present your lover a gift (which should be gift-wrapped) while the two of you are waiting in the back seat of the limo.

Again, this should be a surprise, and it will be a day they will remember forever.

If you own a canoe or row-boat, you're in business, if not, you can rent one. Either way, take a picnic basket full of your lover's favorite food, a guitar if you play one; if not, a small stereo and some tapes of old love songs will do just fine.

Then day or night, depending on whether you wish to bask in the sun or romance by moonlight, put your miniature love boat in a nearby lake or pond and begin your cruise.

Some ideas for the love cruise are:

(A) As you leave the shoreline, take the guitar or tape player out and start singing love songs to your lover. If you have the talent to write your own love song do so, and sing it to them.

If you're not musically inclined, you can write a poem saying how much they mean to you and read it to them while the soft music from the stereo plays in the background.

(B) Paddle to a remote area on the lake, (such as an isolated island) or a place along the shore where the two of you will be alone, build a fire to sit by, and spread a blanket on the ground so you can enjoy a romantic picnic.

(C) You can bring sleeping bags and camping equipment, and raft down the river or lake and spend the night out in the woods.

The two of you can cuddle up, look at the star-filled heavens, and tell how much each or you really means to the other.

Ideas such as these are very inexpensive, so practically anyone can enjoy them. The main thing is they are romantic and sure to fill your lover's heart with a sense of romance.

On the next stormy night, have an inside picnic with your lover for a romantic time together.

Set up a picnic table, or lay a blanket and a couple of pillows on the floor next to a large window at home. If the wind isn't blowing too much, open up the window to allow the fresh smell of the rain to fill the room.

This should be done by candlelight (to add to the atmosphere) and on the table, or blanket, have a picnic basket full of your mate's favorite foods, some grapes to hand feed them, a bottle of wine, (or grape juice if you prefer non-alcoholic beverages) and plenty or snacks to last for the duration.

Have the stereo playing in the background with some rainy-day songs like, "RAINDROPS KEEP FALLING ON MY HEAD", "SINGING IN THE RAIN", "RAININ' IN MY HEART", OR "LET IT RAIN, LET IT RAIN".

Once you have everything in place, just enjoy your rainy night together. It's romantic!

You can give your lover a surprise picnic by using this idea. Pack up an ice-chest full of all the picnic supplies you'll need. Pack the wine or juices, the sandwich spread, the bread, etc.

Once you have everything ready, go to a nice park, take the trash can liner out of one of the trash barrels, place the ice chest in the bottom of the barrel, then put the plastic liner back in place, covering your ice-chest and hiding it from everyone.

Later that day, you say to your lover, "Let's go for a walk in the park." On your walk, you of course stop by the trash can, uncover the ice-chest, and surprise your lover with an instant picnic.

You can even go more all out on your picnic surprise by giving your lover a first class picnic dinner. You plan this in advance and have a tablecloth spread either on the ground, or on a picnic table in the park. On the tablecloth you have the candles and flowers, fine china, the whole works. You can even hire a band to play soft romantic music in the background if you'd like.

You ask your lover to visit the park with you, and when you drive up, there it is!

Take an ice-chest packed full of your lover's favorite foods and drinks, gift wrap it, then have it delivered to your lover at their work.

With the gift wrapped chest, have a nice card saying something like, "For the time of your life, bring this package and meet me at (the time you wish to meet) at (the place you desire) and you'll have it!" Then be there waiting for your lover.

The time should be for their lunch break, or, after work for dinner. The place can be at a nearby park and the two of you can have a picnic. Or a busy street corner close to their work will do. A chauffeur-driven limousine will pull up, the chauffeur will get out and open the rear door for your lover, and they'll find you sitting, waiting, and ready to enjoy a ride around town while the two of you feast on the food and drinks from the ice-chest.

Call your lover up at work early in the work day. Ask if the two of you can have lunch, and when they accept your invitation, tell them what time to be expecting you.

Instead of showing up and taking them out to lunch, show up with a picnic basket full of food, a tablecloth, cold drinks, two of your finest plates from the china cabinet, your best silverware, a candelabra, flowers for the table, and a small stereo with a tape of soft romantic music.

If your mate works behind a desk, clear off half the desk, spread the tablecloth on the cleared area, set out the candelabra and the flowers, light the candles, put out the china and silver, turn on the tape, propose a toast to the two of you, and enjoy a romantic lunch right there at the work place.

If they don't have a desk job, there may be a lounge where the workers have lunch and you can set up shop at one of the lounge tables. If not, then the two of you can go outside and spread the tablecloth on the ground.

Any one of the three will be a lunch they won't soon forget and will be much more romantic than taking them to the nearest cafe for a regular lunch break.

You can take this idea as far as you would like. You can add to the romance of the idea by wearing a tuxedo, emptying a champagne bottle of the real stuff and filling it with juice, hiring someone to come in and play music as the two of you enjoy your lunch, or even hiring someone to serve as a waiter for the two of you.

Instead of carrying in the picnic lunch, you can even have the lunch catered if you prefer. Whatever you decide, it will be fun for the both of you.

A sure way to romance your lover is to have a dinner at their favorite place to dine, but in this case, it should be prearranged by you.

Go to their favorite place, talk to the owner or manager, and tell them just what you have in mind. Set the date for your dinner with the management and make certain every detail is covered in advance.

When you arrive for the dinner, there should be a reserved table waiting for you with flowers, long tapered candles, and your lover's favorite wine or champagne. The waiter will then seat you and serve the drinks.

Since the dinner has been prearranged by you, you don't have to order anything at all. After the drinks have been poured, the waiter will bring out the appetizers; then, when the main course is served, the waiter will bring your lover their favorite dish, or maybe something they have always wanted to try, but never have.

In short, the two of you should be treated as royalty, and it will be a romantic evening your lover will remember always.

Mark and Sally had been dating for some time and had dinner together most every night. Most often, they dined out, but on occasion, Sally would cook dinner and have Mark over for a home-cooked meal. Mark decided to return the favor.

Mark set up a lovely dinner table in his back yard, complete with red and white checked tablecloths, fresh cut flowers, long tapered candles, his best china and silverware, (which you can rent if you don't own) and a four post awning (such as campers use to cover picnic tables) in case of inclimate weather.

He had outdoor torches burning just outside the four corners of the awning to give off a romantic glow, as well as to help control the insects.

Mark had a good friend act as a waiter, and when Sally arrived, she was seated, served champagne, then the appetizers. The main course was rolled out on a cart under bell-covers, served by the waiter in a tuxedo. Then came the dessert and more drinks.

After dinner, there was loving conversation and a walk around the yard to gaze at the stars overhead. Then Sally and Mark danced to the sounds of the soft music flowing from the stereo Mark had placed close by.

It turned out to be an evening both Sally and Mark will never forget, and you can have the same type of evening with your lover. All it takes to enjoy such an evening is a backyard and a little imagination.

If you desire, you can prepare the meal yourself, or if you prefer, you can have the meal catered to your backyard. You can even go more all out than Mark by hiring someone to play the music and enjoy live entertainment.

If you live in an area where the law allows it, you may want to build a fire in or around a pit in your yard, and after dinner, the two of you can enjoy your drinks and conversation by the fire.

The extent of this all-out back-yard dinner is completely up to you and the ideas are limitless. Use your own imagination and give your lover a dinner which is special in every way.

It matters not if you're dating, living together, or married, the two of you will be in a romantic mood after such an evening.

♡ (135) A Private Night Out

Give your lover a private night out by talking to the owner of their favorite place to dine and renting the entire restaurant for a couple of hours so you and your lover will be the only customers.

If you don't have the money to rent out the entire establishment, you can rent out a whole banquet room or a private booth with curtains secluding the two of you from the other clientele.

You can do the same thing at a local theater to treat your mate to a private showing of a new movie they have been wanting to see.

Once you have made the arrangements with the owner or management, hire a violinist to play for the two of you while you enjoy your romantic dinner, or to serenade you before the private showing of the movie.

A setting such as this is perfect for proposing marriage, celebrating a special day in your lives, or just saying "I love you and want to show you how special you are to me"!

♡ (136) A Formal Wedding Proposal

Larry and Nancy had been dating for some time, both were truly in love, and Larry decided it was time he ask the big question of Nancy. He was going to ask her to marry him.

He wanted it to be a special proposal and he thought of several different ways to go about it. He made a decision that he would like for the proposal to be a formal affair, so here's what he did.

He bought her a beautiful engagement ring, then went to a print-shop and had a special menu printed. The menu he had made looked just like the ones from Nancy's favorite place to dine, with one exception. On the bottom of the inside page of the

120

menu, it said, "The special of the day is, "Will you marry me?"

He then rented himself a tuxedo, and bought Nancy a beautiful formal evening gown and heels to match. He had the gown and shoes gift wrapped and attached a nice card with a message written inside.

Larry then took the special menu, gift-wrapped present, and a dozen red roses to the restaurant Nancy loved so well, talked to the manager to apprise him of his plans, then talked to the waiter who would serve them that evening so he would know exactly what to do and say. He then made his reservations and left the items for Nancy, as well as his tuxedo, with the waiter.

That evening he picked Nancy up to go out to dinner and when they arrived, his plans worked to perfection. The hostess seated them at one of the regular tables and left two regular menus for them. Once they were seated and looking over the menu, Larry asked if she would excuse him for a moment while he went to the men's room. As soon as Larry was out of sight, the waiter came to the table and said, "I'm so sorry, but we have made a mistake. This isn't the table where you are to be. Would you follow me to your correct table please?"

Nancy followed him to a room that was normally a banquet room, and that night, it was set for the occasion. Candlelight, soft romantic music playing in the background, iced down champagne, and the gift-wrapped present from Larry were awaiting Nancy as the waiter seated her once more.

Larry was in the manager's office changing into his tuxedo as Nancy read the card attached to the gift. It said, "I thought I would surprise you with a very formal romantic dinner and you might like to dress for the occasion. Please change and meet me here in ten minutes. Love Larry."

Nancy opened her gift, saw the beautiful gown and heels, and went to the ladies room to change into them. Larry met her at the entrance to the special room they had set for them and escorted her back to the table once she had changed.

Nancy asked, somewhat bewilderedly,"What is going on?" Larry's only reply was, "You ain't seen nothing yet!"

Once they were both seated and in their formal attire, the waiter poured the champagne for them and Larry proposed a fitting toast to the two of them.

The waiter left only briefly for them to enjoy their drinks, then returned with a cart carrying a silver bell-cover and the special menu Larry had had printed.

He gave the special menu to Nancy and said, "There are quite a few items on the menu that I think you will find to your liking, but may I point out that the special of the day is Larry would like to know if you will marry him, Nancy."

At the same time the waiter was delivering his message to her, Nancy was reading Larry's proposal on the menu herself. The waiter then opened the bell-cover, which was covering the dozen roses. Larry took the roses and presented them to Nancy and asked, "Well, will you marry me?"

Nancy immediately said "Yes!" and Larry took out the engagement ring, placed it on her finger, gave her a passionate kiss, and said, "I love you and want to be with you forever!"

The remainder of the evening was spent enjoying the most romantic meal they had ever had together, then dancing to the love songs which were playing in the background.

It was a formal affair, (just as Larry wanted) and one of the most romantic that either of them could have ever imagined.

(137) The Restaurant of Love

To put this idea into motion, go to a printer and have a special menu printed. Have a pleasing looking cover made with designs of hearts, roses, and maybe the figure of Cupid drawing back his bow on it. At the top of the menu's cover, have the name "THE RESTAURANT OF LOVE" printed.

Inside the menu will be listed special romantic dinners with the suggested price.

EXAMPLE:
STEAK DINNER WITH TWO VEGETABLES AND SALAD--- A BACK RUB
LOBSTER DINNER WITH ALL THE TRIMMINGS--- HUGS AND KISSES

PORK CHOPS WITH TWO VEGETABLES AND SALAD--- A FOOT MASSAGE

These are only examples and your menu can include any item you would like, but make sure they are your lover's favorite meals.

Once your menu is printed up, send it to your lover at work or at their home by special carrier. After you know they have received the menu, call them up and say, "This is (your name) and I'm calling for "THE RESTAURANT OF LOVE" to take your order for dinner tonight." Then you add, "I would like to point out that the prices listed are only suggested prices and are strictly negotiable."

Once they have placed their order and told you what time they would prefer to dine, you can go buy the food and prepare the meal yourself, or have someone come in to prepare the meal for you.

The place where you set up "THE RESTAURANT OF LOVE" should be made to look as much like a restaurant as possible. Whether it be your home, your lover's home, or a hotel room, try to find a location with a nice view. Set the dinner table up right next to the window, lay out a red and white checkered tablecloth, with candles and flowers on it, and have the lap napkins and salt and pepper shakers in place. In other words, try to make it look as realistic as possible.

When your lover shows up for the dinner, the food should be ready, and you should hire someone to serve the dinner to you and your lover and to clean up afterwards.

Once the dinner is complete, you collect the price of the meal be it the hugs and kisses, the foot massage, etc. Try it; you and your lover will both enjoy the evening.

Invite your lover over for dinner and have the perfect atmosphere set for the evening. Have soft lights, (such as a candelabra) soft music playing in the background, checkered red and white tablecloths on the table, and your best china and silverware, which you can rent. Then serve the food just as would be done if the two of you had gone out to dine. This type of atmosphere makes it a special evening.

If you have a fireplace, you can have a fire going and the table set in the same room as the fireplace.

While the two of you wait for dinner to be served, have champagne served, propose a suitable toast, and enjoy romantic conversation with your lover.

To add even more class to the occasion, you can hire a caterer to cook and serve you, (they will also clean up after dinner), and you can hire someone to come in and play the violin at table side. Or if you have a piano, have someone come in and play old love songs for the two of you during the dinner.

You can also add some of your own ideas that you know your lover would enjoy, and romance will fill the air.

For a romantic evening at home that your lover will appreciate and remember, come home early one day and prepare his or her favorite dinner.

Build a fire in the fireplace, lay a big bear-skin rug in front of the fire, then set the table just behind the rug. Have the table complete with red and white tablecloth, fine china, silverware, flowers, candelabra,and chilled wine or champagne. On the rug, you should have a basket of grapes that you can hand-feed your lover as you lie in front of the romantic fire. The lights should be off so you can place candles about to give the room a romantic glow. There should also be soft romantic music coming from the stereo.

When your lover gets home from work, be waiting at the door with the room set up and ready for your evening. Escort them to the bear-skin rug and begin the evening with a nice long foot rub followed by a complete body massage.

Hand feed your mate the grapes while they enjoy their drink of wine or champagne in front of the fire, then seat them at the table and serve the dinner you have prepared just for them.

Once the dinner is over, dance to the music from the stereo, return to the rug, enjoy the fire, then have a cover nearby so the two of you can cover and cuddle up to spend the night right there on the floor.

Don't worry about the mess from dinner! It will still be there for you to clean up the next day, and the romantic evening you and your lover will enjoy should not be interrupted by anyone or anything, especially not by cleaning!

♡ 140 Breakfast in Bed

Show your lover how much you care for them by doing little unexpected things for them from time to time.

One thing you can do to show you are always considerate of them is to serve breakfast in bed on a day when they certainly don't expect anything special from you.

You can get up an hour earlier than usual, fix their favorite breakfast, serve it on a tray with a single rose, and pour their breakfast juice from a wine or champagne bottle you have emptied of the real stuff and filled with their favorite juice.

If they work, have a warm bath drawn for them to enjoy after their breakfast, then have the clothes they are to wear that day laid out for them, pressed and ready.

You may choose to hire someone to come in and prepare breakfast for the two of you; then you can enjoy the breakfast as well while lying right along side your lover.

If you have a bedroom fireplace, it would add to the atmosphere to have a fire going. If you don't have a bedroom fireplace, you can place some candles about to add a romantic touch.

It's the little unexpected things such as breakfast in bed that keep the love fires burning in your affair or marriage just as hot as they were the day the two of you realized you were truly in love.

Gentlemen, if you really want to surprise your lover, make reservations for a romantic dinner on the day of the big game. (Such as the Super Bowl).

Don't tip her off beforehand and let her think you're going to be right in front of the television during the game.

Have the dinner reservations made for just about kick-off time, and just before the game comes on the air, ask her if she would like to go out to dinner.

True love calls for sacrifice from time to time, and this would be the perfect time to show your lover that she is more important to you than any sporting event (or anything else) could ever be.

She has probably been dreading the hour of the kick-off wondering what she could do to occupy herself while you enjoyed the game. This is the answer and it will thrill her! And after all, you can set the V.C.R. and watch the game at a later date.

The true romantic thinks of the little things such as this and it makes for a stronger relationship between the partners.

(142) Hot Air Balloons

To give your lover a special morning, rent a hot air balloon for a balloon ride over your town with a champagne brunch set up on board.

Many cities have these hot air balloon services and many specialize in romantic settings for your ride.

If you live near the beach, a lake, or river, you can enjoy the champagne brunch on your ride to the shoreline, then have a boat ride as the hot air balloon pulls you and your lover along by a cable from the balloon to the boat.

It will be an enjoyable day for your mate and a romantic way for you to say "I love you!"

(143) You Are Cordially Invited

A very romantic way to ask that special someone in your life out for an evening is to send them a formal invitation.

First, buy one of the wooden gift boxes containing a bottle of champagne and two glasses, then purchase a formal invitation card and fill it out.

Where the card says "You are cordially invited to", you put, "A romantic evening with me!" Where it says, "at", you fill in the place you would like for them to meet you, and in the place for the time, you will of course fill in the time they are to be there. In the R.S.V.P. space, put in your phone number, (just in case they can't make it) and at the bottom of the card write the letters B.Y.O.B. (for bring your own bottle—which will be the champagne you will send them) and sign the card.

Place the formal invitation inside the wooden gift box with the champagne and glasses, gift wrap it, and have it delivered to that special person.

The place they are to meet you for the romantic evening can

be anywhere you desire. It can be at a local restaurant for dinner, a hotel, mountain or lake cabin, your house, or just a park bench or table in a nearby park.

Where and what you have in mind should be planned well in advance. For instance, if you choose the restaurant or hotel, have reservations. If you choose to meet at one of the cabins or your home, have everything ready you will need to provide the romantic evening promised. If it's to be the park where they will meet you, have a picnic basket full of foods they love and grapes to hand feed your date.

It's fun, it's romantic, and you'll both have a great time!

⟨144⟩ A First Class Lunch

Take a day, or at least half a day off from work for this idea. If your lover works, call up their supervisor and tell them what you have planned. Tell them you would like for the plan to be a surprise to your lover and when your mate comes in to ask for the day, or half day off, (whichever you have planned) not to tip them off to the fact you've already made arrangements for them to be off.

Call your lover at work and say you'd like to take them some place special for lunch and have them ask their supervisor for the afternoon off (which you have seen to already).

Have the reservations you will need made in advance, pick your lover up at work, then drive to the airport, park the car, and fly off to enjoy a first-class lunch. Some ideas for the lunch are:

(A) Fly to New York for some Coney Island Hot-Dogs or Cheese Cake.

(B) Fly to Chicago for some famous Chicago Pizza or Chicago Dogs.

(C) Fly to Philadelphia for Submarine Sandwiches.

(D) Fly to New Orleans for Cajun food.

(E) Fly to Baltimore for Seafood.

Once the lunch is over, the two of you fly home.

(145) A Little Romance at McDonald's

The next time you and your lover are going out to a fast-food restaurant, such as a McDonald's, Wendy's, Burger King, etc. plan in advance and use this to surprise and romance your mate.

Have some wild flowers and a candle in the back of the car. Once you have ordered and the two of you are seated, go to the car, get them out, place them on the table, light the candle, and have a romantic dinner at the fast food restaurant.

Your lover will enjoy it and marvel at how clever your are when it comes to romancing them.

(146) Reservations at a Fast Food Restaurant

Set this up with the manager of the fast food restaurant that you and your lover eat at quite often. Talk to the manager to let them know just what time you and your mate will show up. Have them greet you at the door just as you would be greeted at an expensive place to dine. They will then act as if they are checking the reservation list and say, "Oh yes, here it is. Mr. Lawson. Reservations for two."

The manager will then escort you and your mate to a table they have set up for you with the items you brought in when you set the whole thing up with them.

On the table will be a red and white checkered tablecloth, a dozen red roses, a candelabra, and an ice bucket with a bottle of chilled grape juice (since there are no alcoholic beverages allowed in these establishments).

Once the manager has seated you, they will give you and your lover a menu to order from. The menu will be a fancy one just like you would get at an expensive place, so you will have to have had it made up in advance.

During the entire dinner, the management will treat you like royalty, so you will have to leave a very nice tip for the trouble they have gone to for your romantic fast food dinner.

♡147 *Fly It In*

If you really want to go all out and impress your lover, order an expensive dinner from one of the finest restaurants in Paris or Rome and have it flown to you.

Once the dinner for two has arrived, set up your place in the most romantic setting imaginable, thaw the food one afternoon, and have the fantastic romantic meal with the romantic aura surrounding you and your lover. You may wish to decorate the room to look like Paris, France or Rome, Italy; it will add a little flavor to the occasion.

You could also hire one of the famous chefs of the world for an evening, have them come in and prepare the meal of your choice, then have the romantic dinner served to the two of you in that same romantic setting.

One way or the other, you're sure to impress on your lover the fact that you are willing to go all out and that nothing is too good for them. You give the message that dinner with them is not just another dinner. It's something special.

148 The Ultimate Romantic Evening

To put this plan into motion, have a bottle of chilled champagne delivered to your lover with two glasses decorated with red curled ribbons. Have a note attached to the bottle saying you will pick them up at a certain time,and asking them to keep the champagne chilled and to have it with them when you arrive.

When the hour arrives, have a chauffeur enter their place of work, or home, (depending on where you are to pick them up) with a dozen roses and a gift-wrapped box containing a nice present.

The chauffeur will then escort your mate to the waiting limousine, where you will be waiting for them. The driver will then head to the airport while the two of you enjoy the champagne.

The entire evening's events will be a surprise to your lover, so they will have no idea where the two of you are going. Once you have reached the airport, a helicopter will be waiting to fly you and your lover to a romantic spot you have picked out in advance.

An ideal place for the helicopter to land would be a field near a lake, mountain or ocean Also nice would be a high elevation overlooking a nice view, or some other suitable romantic location.

When the helicopter lands, you should have a band near the landing spot playing music for the two of you to enjoy. There should be a table and two chairs with the table complete with red and white tablecloth, flowers, candelabra, and fine china and silverware.

A waiter will escort you and your lover from the landing site to the table, allow the two of you time to enjoy the music, then serve the dinner.

Once your dinner is over, you and your lover can take a walk around the location, sit by an outdoor fire to enjoy the view, listen to more romantic music being played by the band, then have the limousine pick you up and take you to a nice hotel (where you will spend the rest of the evening).

The dinner itself should be a catered affair so everything will be cleaned up for you; so this evening should be planned well in advance. Pick out the location, hire the caterers, band,

133

limousine service, and helicopter a few days before this big event.

The ultimate romantic evening can be the perfect setting to propose marriage, celebrate an anniversary, birthday, etcetera, or just for the fun of it.

CHAPTER SEVEN
AN ASSORTMENT OF IDEAS ON
ROMANCE

This chapter covers many areas of romance. The ideas are various and cover things like first dates, what romance really is, how to seize each romantic opportunity, how to entice your lover, private times with your mate, and many more. Each of these ideas will help you make the relationship you have with your lover a truly romantic one.

149 *I Don't Like It, But I'll Do It.*

To show your love from time to time, and to be a true romantic, you must sacrifice your own feelings for those of your lover. Real love is not unyeilding! Real love is caring more for the well being of the one you love than you do for your own.

In any relationship, there are things one likes that the other doesn't particularly care for. To show you do love that special someone in your life, on occasion, do some of those things you know they enjoy doing that you don't; and do them with a smile on your face with no complaining.

Once you have given them the satisfaction of doing what they desire of you, don't throw it up to them and say things like, "Well I went to church with you, didn't I?" (Or whatever it was you did).

The idea is to do it just as if you really enjoyed it and they will enjoy it more. THAT'S LOVE!

⟨150⟩ Don't Forget the Little Things

Lots of times a love life grows stale only because we overlook the small things, the things most of us take for granted.

Everyone, and I repeat, EVERYONE! loves to be complimented from time to time. Don't forget to compliment your lover on occasion about a new outfit, (how great it looks on her) a new hair style, (how sexy she looks with it) or just her everyday things she does for you, such as, making you dinner or keeping house. The things we never give a second thought about in most cases.

A few things you can remember to do to make your lover feel needed, wanted, and appreciated are:

(A) Never forget to give her a good-bye kiss as you're leaving for work or wherever.

(B) Once in awhile, let her sleep in and you get the children off to school or to the Saturday morning ballgame, etc.

(C) You prepare dinner and clean up afterwards to give them a break.

The list could go on and on, but the thing is to think about the things you may consider too small to worry over and concentrate on remembering they may not be so small an item to your mate. Don't forget the little things and help her out from time to time.

There are times in everyone's life that they need a little something extra from their lover. For a woman, those times come during pregnancy, and even after the child has come.

In most cases, it doesn't take anything big to satisfy your lover; just a small act is needed and appreciated from time to time.

She tends to the newborn child on a twenty-four-hour-a-day basis, and though you may not consider it romantic, it is very romantic to your wife for you to volunteer to help out with the baby.

Think of how much she would love it if the next time the baby woke up crying at 3:00 A.M. you said, "Just go back to sleep honey, I'll take care of it."

That's a small act, but one she'll love you for. Other small acts you could do for her are mixing the formula on occasion, feeding the baby once in awhile, changing the diapers, and even doing the baby's laundry for her.

She's at a period in her life when she really needs you to show you care! So do it! She'll see it as the most romantic thing you could do for her right now.

152 Simple Little Romantic Moments

Romantic moments in yours and your lover's life don't always have to be big, all out, expensive adventures. There are all kinds of simple little things which are just as romantic as anything you could ever dream up.

For example, take your lover out to a park at night and swing them on the children's swings under the stars. Take them on a hayride in the back of an old truck in the cool of the fall. Take them on a sleigh ride this winter. Take them sledding in the snow and after a long shoot down a steep hill, hug each other to warm up next to a big fire. Have a wiener-roast in the back yard on a cool evening for just the two of you.

Take your lover out to fly a kite on a windy afternoon. Though you can propose marriage on any of these little romantic moments, (and turn the little moments into huge ones) flying the kite can be a special one. You paint the message, "Will you marry me?" on the kite, and when it's airborne, your lover sees your proposal.

If you're not ready to take that step just yet, you can still add a touch of romance to the already romantic moment by writing, "I love you!" on the kite.

153 Seize the Opportunities

There are all kinds of opportunities afforded us to turn common everyday occurrences into romantic happenings. For instance, Greg and Melinda had been dating for awhile, and one morning Melinda called to say she had lost the clasp to one of her earrings. She asked Greg to keep it for her if he happened to find it.

Greg searched the carpet, the chair Melinda sat in the night before, and finally found it in the seat of his car. He could have easily put the clasp away until he saw her later that evening, but he took the chance given him and turned it into a romantic gesture.

What Greg did was to send Melinda a dozen red roses with a nice card. He had them delivered to her at work. He taped the lost clasp inside the card, and wrote nothing at all. The clasp itself was all that was on the card.

Melinda thought that was very romantic and it certainly brightened what would have otherwise been a regular day.

True romantics seize each opportunity afforded them and make the life of their lover a little brighter each day. So seize those opportunities; your lover will love it!

(154) The Fortune Cookie

Linda found out she was expecting her first child. She had been to the doctor and he confirmed her suspicions that she was indeed pregnant.

She couldn't wait to tell her husband Mike the wonderful news. She thought about the perfect way to share the excitement and came up with this idea. She went to a local Chinese restaurant where Mike loved to eat from time to time. She talked to the manager, told him her plan, then made reservations for that evening.

The manager took one of the fortune cookies they served with each meal, took a pair of tweezers, and removed the fortune note from the cookie. Linda then typed the following note, "We did it Honey! I'm pregnant and the baby is due in seven months!"

She and the manager then took pains to place Linda's note inside the fortune cookie, and the manager kept her cookie in his jacket pocket.

That evening, after the meal, the Manager placed the fortune cookies on the table. Linda read her fortune first. It was a regular fortune cookie and said something similar to all fortune cookies. Then Mike read his out loud, realized what was happening, and was thrilled. He jumped up, hugged and kissed Linda, and when he had finally settled down from his excitement, he marveled at her ingenuity in announcing her pregnancy.

It was exciting news and Linda came up with an exciting way of telling Mike about it. You can do the same with your lover. You don't have to be expecting a child to do this. You can place any message inside you wish to.

You can ask that special someone to marry you, say happy birthday or anniversary, or if you have no special day or announcements to make, you can just say how much you love them.

No matter what note you place inside the fortune cookie, it will surprise them to find it's a personal note inside as opposed to the standard note, and they will remember it forever.

(155) Recall Your First Date

After you have been dating—or married—for awhile, say five years or more, you can use this idea to bring back some fond memories and excite your lover.

Put your first date together in a real life, instant replay by reliving it from start to finish.

Think about the first time the two of you went out, where you went, what you did, what you had to eat, the people you were with, etc. Then, go to the same places, do the same things, have the same meal, and invite those same people to share the evening with the two of you. As much as your total recall will allow, even carry on the same conversations. It will be interesting to see if you still think as you did about the small things in life that you talked about back then.

One thing's for sure, both you and your lover will enjoy the evening. After all, you both enjoyed it so much the first go-round that you're still together!

141

After you've been married for awhile, the last thing in the world your wife expects is for you to ask her for a date. However, that doesn't mean she wouldn't love the romantic notion of it.

One day, just on a whim, take an extra set of clothes to work with you, (without your wife knowing about it) then call her up at lunch time and ask her if the two of you can go out on a date that evening. Be sure and use the word "date!" She will of course say yes, and you're on your way to igniting the flame of love that may be dwindling to a flicker after a few years of marriage.

Have reservations for a romantic dinner as well as reservations for the honeymoon suite at a nearby hotel.

After dinner, you can take her to a play, concert, movie, or some place special she's been wanting to go, (such as a local comedy club).

After the night on the town, you go to the honeymoon suite, where there are a dozen roses, a bottle of champagne, and a midnight snack there for the two of you to enjoy in a romantic setting

Then you enjoy lounging in the hot-tub together before carrying her to the bed for the night. On the bed you'll have a gift waiting for her, such as a necklace around the neck of a Teddy-Bear with a note saying how much you're in love.

Next morning, shower, change into the extra set of clothes, and let her sleep in as you leave for work. On your lunch break, return to have your lunch with your wife, drive her home after the lunch, and as you leave to return to work for the afternoon, give her a nice card saying how much you enjoyed the date, how much you love her, and how you would like another date with her real soon.

Along with the card you can give her a glass-blown baby grand piano, (in a gift-wrapped box) and the closing line on your written message can be "I HAD A GRAND TIME!"

Romance thrives! It lives in all of us. The want, as well as the need for romance is inside us all. But in these busy times, it just doesn't come out as often as it once did.

Since we all do indeed desire and reqiure a little romance from time to time, sometimes all it takes to get it going is a little enticement.

To fan the flames of love, and to get the romantic juices flowing in your lover, leave them notes of enticement from time to time and you'll be amazed at the results.

One example of an enticinq note that works is to invite your mate to a romantic evening with you by leaving a note where they will be certain to find it (like on the windshield of their car) which says, "You bring the wine, I'll start the fire!" The fire in this case, of course, is the romantic fire which burns inside us.

If you take the initiative and leave that first note of enticement for your lover, you'll be surprised at how well it works. So don't be shocked if next time your lover leaves one for you to find.

If, after awhile, the luster seems to be wearing off your relationship, it could be because of the sameness in the relationship day after day after day!

Kelly and Ryan had been married for only a short while, but as the old saying goes, the honeymoon was over. They loved each other and there was no doubt about it. But there seemed to be very few new and exciting moments in their relationship. Kelly decided to do something about it.

One night, after dinner, Kelly cleaned off the dinner table then went to the bedroom. She had placed the dishes in the sink to be washed, dried, and put away. She then changed clothes and put on a surprise outfit to do the dishes in.

She slipped back into the kitchen, then asked Ryan, who had gone into the den to read the evening paper, if he would help her with the dishes.

When he entered the kitchen to help, there was Kelly in black underwear, garter-belt, fish-net stockings, and high-heels.

She was enticing her man, and needless to say, it worked! Kelly was doing something different to add some excitement to their lives.

Ryan loved helping her with the dishes, and loved her idea of enticement.

If your relationship seems to have settled into a dull existence, try to entice your lover; you'll profit from the end result.

159 Entice Your Lover (Part II)

There are all kinds of ways to entice your mate to spend their time with you instead of idlely passing it in front of the television. Carroll got tired of her husband Greg's normal weekend routine of passing his day watching the baseball game on T.V., so she did something about it.

Their son was a catcher on one of the local Little League teams and his outfit was in his bedroom closet. Carroll put on her son's chest protector, shin-guards, catcher's mask, and catcher's mit, and underneath the baseball gear, she wore absolutely nothing.

She came down the stairs to the den, (where Greg was tuned in to the ballgame) jumped in front of the television, and yelled, "Let's play ball!"

It certainly got Greg's attention; and needless to say, he got the idea.

This is just an example of how one person let her lover know it was time for something romantic to happen in their lives, and that there is more to weekends than ballgames.

Excite your lover by doing something similar to this. If you entice your lover from time to time, you'll both be grateful for the effort.

*

⟨160⟩ *Hot Oils and Lotions*

One romantic idea that your lover will never get enough of is a complete body massage with hot oils and lotions. It just feels good! Not only that, it's soothing, relaxing, and sure to set the tone of the evening at a fevered romantic pitch.

Take some regular body lotion and skin oils, mix them in a container which can be placed in the microwave, then heat them to the point that they are hot, but not so hot the body can't take it.

Have the bedroom set in a romantic aura with candlelight, and even a bottle of champagne or wine if you'd like. If you have a fireplace, you may wish to give the hot oil and lotion massage in front of the romantic fire. If not, the bed will work just as well.

Begin the body massage by going from head to toe. Pause on occasion to enjoy a glass of wine, talk about romantic things and ideas the two of you would like to try, then continue to massage.

Once you have exhausted the supply of oils and lotions you have heated up in the microwave, the romantic mood has been set. Just enjoy the rest of the evening with your lover.

⟨161⟩ *A Candlelight Bath*

One evening when you're in a romantic mood and want to put your lover in that same frame of mind, fill the tub with a sweet smelling bubble-bath, bath oils, and a few floating roses. Then light lots of candles (at least a dozen or more) and place them around the bathroom.

When your lover comes home from work, help them undress, lead them to the candlelight bath, and bathe each other from head to toe.

This idea tends to affect and arouse both you and your lover's desires and should be the beginning of a memorable evening.

To add a little to the romantic occasion, you may choose to have a bottle of wine or champagne iced down to enjoy during the bath.

A different way to acheive the same result is to leave a note on the front door for your lover to meet you in the bathroom, while you are waiting in the tub.

162 A Short Autobiography About Your Life Together

A lasting gift which is unique is an autobiography about how your own life has gone since that wonderful day you met your lover for the first time and realized they were your dream person.

The first step in doing this is to take a surprise picture of your lover. By surprise picture, I mean a candid shot catching them off guard; snap a picture when they're not expecting it.

Once you have your picture, you make up a little funny story that the off-guard pose might inspire in you. Look at the picture carefully and see if it might suggest what was going through your lover's mind at the time it was snapped, then write the funny lines to go with it.

Once you have written the funny part, get serious. Write a few pages about the two of your lives together. Go back to when you first met, when you first realized you were indeed in love, to when you knew for certain that they loved you too, and continue the story in an autobiography about your life with your dream lover. Cover everything you can think of from the day you met right on up to the day you write the short story.

Once you have finished, you can take the picture, funny short story about the picture, and autobiography to a printer and have them put it in a book form for you. Or, you can type the stories out, place them in a folder, glue or tape the picture in front, and present your lover with a homemade book.

Homemade or professionally printed, your lover will have a lasting gift that they will treasure forever.

If you have children, you already know how scarce the time is for you and your husband or wife to be alone in the house without an interruption by those children.

All couples, regardless of how long they've been together or how many children they may have to interrupt them, need that private time to be together. They need quiet time to talk, console and comfort each other, and attain the self assurance that they are indeed still the number one thing in each other's life.

Even though it may be hard to accomplish at times, there is a way, and you need to make certain you and your mate have those private times on every occasion possible.

One way is to go about it the way Jean did with her husband Steve. She made certain each of the children was occupied with something that would keep them so for awhile. She left a note on the kitchen table, where Steve would easily find it, which said, "Meet me in the bathroom at 8:00 P.M. for a private little get together."

She had a warm bath drawn. Candlelight flickered and danced from the walls and ceiling, setting a romantic tone, and she had a bottle of wine cooled for the occasion.

She accomplished just what she set out to do. She and Steve had their private time together and enjoyed every moment of it. By finding these times together from time to time, their relationship remains strong and secure.

Follow Jean's lead and find the time to be alone with your mate. Your relationship will be stronger because of your efforts.

(164) Confirming your Love by Phone

Sometimes love is taken for granted and that is a drastic mistake. One way to prevent this from happening is to surprise your partner occasionally with an unexpected phone call.
You call them at a moment when they certainly aren't expecting it, at home or at work (with your surprise message).

Call them up and say, "I was just thinking of you and wanted to tell you I love you more than you will ever know." Or, you may say, "I just wanted to call and say you are the most beautiful person I have ever known!"

You may want to say something private that only the two of you would understand, or something about how lucky you feel to be a part of their life, like, "I was truly lucky to have found a person as wonderful as you."

The main thing is to give them your message and hang up before they even have a chance to reply; that's the idea behind this. Just let them know that you care deeply, that they are indeed on your mind, and you certainly don't take their love for granted.

(165) Morning Rose Petals

One morning, wake up a little earlier than normal and start the day off on a romantic note for your lover.

Spread rose petals from their side of the bed to the bathroom, then have rose petals spread on the bottom of the tub for their shower. Or, draw them a warm bath and have the rose petals floating in the bath.

It's a small act but a romantic notion that your lover will appreciate, and the small act will keep you on their mind for the remainder of the day.

150

(166) Special Times on the Beach

A walk on the beach is always romantic, and anytime seems to be the right time. There are so many romantic notions that a stroll along the beach inspires in a person.

Just picture you and your lover as you walk along the shoreline, holding hands, chatting about nothing in particular as the sand goes sifting through your toes with each step.

Think about the cool ocean salt water swishing against your legs with its cooling effect on a hot summer day or evening. Look off in the distance and you see the beautiful sun set with a picture so strikingly beautiful only nature could paint it. How could this be anything but romantic?

Think about the waves rolling in on a sandy beach as you and your lover snuggle on a sand-dune in the moonlight. The fresh smell of nature blows in with an aroma that can never be duplicated nor bottled, and the breeze tosses your lover's hair into a windblown style that's so sexy it can never be reproduced by any hair stylist.

These things, as well as many others, are natural happenings on any beach, but you can bring along a few things to help make the beach an even more romantic spot for you and your lover.

You can spend the night on the beach with your lover and bring along some candles enclosed in a globe so the wind doesn't blow them out. You may choose to bring a lantern instead, or, build a fire (if it's a beach which allows open fires).

Bring along a bottle of wine, some grapes to hand-feed your lover, and even a few snacks to enjoy during the stay. If you plan on staying the entire evening, bring along a couple of sleeping bags or an old blanket to cuddle up in. Then, rise early, and marvel at the sun-rise in the eastern sky that nature has placed on its easel for your viewing enjoyment. That wonderous view will start the day off on a romantic note that will last throughout the day.

There are all types of romantic spots, but to the true romantic, none seems more special than the beach when you can share it with the true love of your life.

⟨167⟩ *Moonlight Feels Right*

On a warm night, when the moonlight is bright, take your lover to the beach, lake, etc. and build a fire for the two of you to enjoy near the water, somewhere along the shoreline.

Talk about the great times of the past, the high hopes for the future, and enjoy a bottle of wine. The first thing you know, the two of you will be in the mood to skinny-dip!

There's nothing more romantic than to skinny-dip with your lover, hold them in your arms while the warm water splashes against the skin, and the bright moonlight beams down on you; it just feels right!

It will feel good for the two of you to just act like kids for awhile. You'll both enjoy the feeling.

⟨168⟩ *Just in Love*

We've all seen the newly-wedded couples driving along with white shoe-polish all over the car spelling out the words "JUST MARRIED." Most times, they are dragging tin-cans behind them and the cans bounce along the pavement making lots of noise.

Well here is an idea you can use to let your lover know you are truly in love with them and want the whole world to know it.

Call them up and make a date for dinner. Tell them what time you will pick them up. Before leaving your house to go after your lover, take white shoe-polish, and all over your car write, "JUST IN LOVE ! " instead of "JUST MARRIED ! "

Tie lots of tin-cans to the bumper of your car, then place the rope with the cans attached in the trunk of the car so your lover won't hear them as you drive up to their house.

When the hour arrives, drive up to your lover's home, take the rope with the cans attached from the trunk and lay them on the pavement.

Knock or ring the door-bell, and when your lover sees what

you have done, they'll be both amazed and pleased.

The two of you get into the car and drive to the restaurant with the tin-cans dragging behind you, with the message written all over your car for one and all to see. Everyone will know that you're just in love, but most importantly, your lover will know it beyond a shadow of a doubt.

(169) A Private Fashion Show

A unique way to give your lover a gift is to call up a local modeling agency and make arrangements for them to bring a few models to a designated location for a private fashion show for your lover.

You can have the fashion show in your home, your lover's home, or at her place of work on a lunch break.

When you have it set up, tell your lover that you have a special surprise for her. The agency people and the models will show up, give the private showing of the latest fashions; then your lover will pick out her favorite item from those modeled.

Once she has picked out the item, the agency will call you to let you know just what your lover likes, and where it may be purchased.

The same day as the fashion show, you go to the establishment, purchase the item for your lover, have it gift wrapped, and have it delivered to her with an attached card which will say, "This is to you just because I love you."

If you prefer, you can give the gift in person over a romantic dinner that evening. One way or the other, it will be a day and gift that your lover will remember always.

(170) Never Enough Kisses

On a cool day (so the chocolate doesn't melt) place candy kisses all over your lover's car while they are at work. On the seat of the car lay a nice card which says, "I could never give you enough kisses!"

Return home, and from their parking space, lay candy kisses all the way to the front door. On the door, attach another card that says, "No kiss in the world is as sweet as yours!"

The following morning you wake up early and place the kisses all over their car once more with a note saying, "These kisses may not last, but yours last forever!"

It's a small thing to do, but your lover will never forget

(171) Hide Them Well

Write your lover several love notes, or letters. Hide them around the house, and hide them well (so they are not so easily found).

Once you have them all hidden, don't say a word about them. Your lover will eventually find one of the letters and it will have a special meaning when they do.

It could take two or three years before all the notes are found, so you should date each one on the day they are written. Each time another is found, and the old date appears, your lover will again get that warm feeling all over that only true love can send over a person.

Leaving little love notes around the house for your lover to find and read is certainly romantic. Some people leave the notes out in the open (such as on the bar or kitchen table) where they are easily found, while some people choose to make the search somewhat more difficult by hiding them in the cookie jar for instance.

The next time you take the notion to write sweet words of love to your mate, leave the note in a unique place. Don't hide the note, but yet, don't leave it out in the open either.

Leave the note in a place they would never suspect it to be, but still, not hidden. Where? Leave your love note on the roll of bathroom tissue in the bathroom. Your lover would never suspect it to be there, but it will still be easily found.

It's as unique a place as you will ever find and sure to be discovered.

(173) A Love Scroll

Write your lover a love letter on a piece of white cloth. Say how much you love them, how you just couldn't make it without them in your life, and how thankful you are for the day you first met.

Once you have said all the things you wish to say, make the letter a scroll by attaching both ends of the cloth to round wooden sticks which are just slightly longer than the width of the cloth.

When you have assembled the scroll, place the top wooden stick over the door facing and tape it in place (so it is fixed and won't fall) and the bottom stick just on top of the front door of the house.

Leave the door slightly ajar so the stick will rest on the door. Once your lover comes home and opens the door, the scroll/love letter will unroll and be hanging there at eye level for them to read.

At the bottom of your scroll you may want to attach a single red rose for your lover; and if you wish, you can add a P.S. to the letter telling them to meet you at a restaurant or hotel at a certain time for a romantic evening together.

(174) A Train Ride to Romance

Trains are not as common as they once were, but they are still romantic, and AMTRAK offers services in cities that are nearby regardless of where you live.

For something different in yours and your lover's lives, call AMTRAK, see where they stop that's close by, then plan an overnight trip for you and your mate on the train.

It will take you back in time and you will both enjoy a romantic trip into the days gone by.

As I said, it's romantic, and you as well as your lover will find the trip well worth the effort for the romance it offers.

(175) A Love Warrant

Most everyone knows a police officer, or has a friend who knows one personally. Call him or her up and tell them what you have in mind. Once they agree to go along with your plan, go to a print shop and have a legal-looking warrant printed up.

On the front of the warrant, have printed, "This is a summons of love!" Inside the warrant, you can write a nice note saying how much you love them, or you can use it to propose by writing, "Will you marry me?"

You can have the police officer serve the warrant to their home or place of work, but if you have it served at work, be certain to call their supervisor in advance and let them know what's going on so they won't be upset about an employee being arrested on the job.

Either way, work or home, once the officer has served the warrant, they then arrest your lover, (your mate won't be upset over the arrest because the warrant is one of love and they'll know you're behind the whole thing) take them to the waiting patrol car, and without saying where the police are taking them, they drive to a nice restaurant or nearby hotel where you are waiting with a gift of flowers for your lover.

(176) Bar Music

If you and your lover frequent a certain bar quite often, surprise them on your next visit by hiring a quartet to stroll over to your seats and sing the song, "YOU'VE LOST THAT LOVING FEELING" to your lover. But, have them substitute the word "GOT" for the original word "LOST" in their barroom rendition.

This is similar to the scene in the movie TOP GUN in which Tom Cruise sang this song to his love interest.

It's a small thing to do for your lover, but they'll enjoy the moment.

(177) *Just Sneak on Over*

Ladies, there is no man so neat that he can't stand a little cleaning up behind him. With this in mind, it's a great idea to sneak over one day while he's at work (without his knowledge of it) and clean his place up for him.

Clean the place from top to bottom. Do the laundry, fold it and put it away, then prepare his favorite dinner. When he arrives home for the evening, have the dinner set with an aura of romance filling the atmosphere. Go all out with the champagne, candlelight, and the sexiest outfit you could ever imagine.

If you prefer, you can hire someone to come in and clean the place, prepare the meal, or both.

If you hire it done or do it yourself, the main thing is the act itself, and the dinner after will not be soon forgotten by your lover.

(178) *A Good Impression*

To impress that special someone you're dating, and to show them just how special they are to you, tell them you will pick them up the next morning to take them to work, as well as pick them up after work to take them to dinner.

Hire a chauffeur-driven limousine, show up at their house at the prescribed time, and have the chauffeur ring the door-bell and escort your lover to the limousine where you are waiting Then the two of you can enjoy breakfast on the ride to work.

That afternoon the chauffeur will roll out a red carpet from the door of your sweetheart's work place to the limousine, escort them to the car once again, and the two of you can enjoy a bottle of champagne as the driver takes you to your reserved dinner.

After dinner the two of you can sit back and enjoy a long ride in the limousine as the driver takes you to the beach, mountains, or some location near the city or town in which you live.

Your lover will be impressed that you thought this much of them and will know for certain that they are indeed special to you.

(179) The Date's in the Bag

When you meet that special someone that you know you've just got to get to know better and want so badly to ask in a unique way for that first date is to buy a bag of dates, have them gift wrapped, attach a nice card, and have them delivered to the new-found interest.

On the card, write, "I'd love a date with you!" Then sign the card and put the phone number where they can reach you.

Once it's delivered, sit back and wait for your call, because such a romantic invitation will be hard for them to pass up.

It doesn't necessarily have to be a first date proposition to use this idea. You can send the gift-wrapped bag of dates and a card to someone you're already seeing if you'd like. You can invite them out for the evening by putting on the card, "How about another date tonight?" Or you can say, "I'd love a date with you tonight!"

Your love interest will adore your unique way of asking them to go out.

(180) Flowers on the First Date

First impressions are always important, as well as lasting. That being the case, on the first date with that someone special, always bring along a dozen red roses.

You can never go wrong in presenting flowers to a woman, so by giving the roses, you're getting off on the right foot.

Once you've gotten off on the right track, the rest is up to you, but keep in mind, we all love romance at heart. So be romantic throughout the evening and your next call will result in that lovely creature saying, "Yes," they would like to see you again.

CHAPTER EIGHT
MY MOST ROMANTIC MOMENT

Writing this book on romantic ideas was a labor of love for me, because I am truly a romantic at heart. I got my ideas from various sources. Some ideas were passed on to me by friends, some were sent to me by people who had heard about me when word got out about the book, but most were dreamed up by me in my own—well, I guess you'd say my own romantic mind. Since I have shared all, or at least most of my romantic ideas and notions with you, I would like to share my most romantic moment with you the reader as well.

My Most Romantic Moment

I was living in St. Louis and had a female roommate who was a dear friend. One day, she introduced me to Cindy. Little did I realize, at the time of the introduction that with this woman— the woman I had just met-I would soon enjoy the most romantic moment of my life.

The physical attraction was there from the beginning. Or at least it was there on my part. She was astoundingly beautiful!

Cindy *is* five-foot-five-inches and about one hundred twenty pounds. She has black silky hair, the face of a cover-girl, and a body that's second to none.

It didn't take long for me to come to the realization that her beauty was so much more than just the physical. Yes—Cindy's beauty went so much farther than skin deep. She had the greatest personality, and possessed an outstanding mind to go along with her outstanding looks. Cindy was (and still is) witty, charming, thoughtful, understanding, Well—you get the idea. What I'm trying to say is she has just about everything you could ever hope to find in a woman.

Cindy and I became fast friends, and my initial physical attraction quickly changed to an all-out total attraction to her. I knew I wanted to get to know her better, was enjoying the times we shared together, and wanted to share even more.

Cindy was a police officer, and on an occasion that she had a few days off, the two of us decided to make the two-hour drive from St. Louis to Hannibal, Missouri to visit the town and see the sights made famous by Mark Twains' Tom Sawyer.

We headed out for Hannibal around ten o'clock in the morning, stopped at a roadside restaurant for a late breakfast, then continued the short trip. During the drive, as well as over our breakfast, our conversation was aimed at getting to know each other just a little better. I found I was intrigued by her, wanted to know everything I could about her, and hoped, as well as felt, that she was feeling the same towards me.

When we arrived in Hannibal, we walked around town, visited the Tom Sawyer house, saw the fence that was white-washed by the boys in town that Tom could con into manning a brush, and enjoyed each moment together.

Just walking around town seeing the tourist attractions felt so good. It just felt right being with Cindy, and to just hold her hand as we walked made me feel good all over and proud to be seen with her.

On our walk we saw an advertisement on a poster-board advertising Hannibal's celebration of the town's bi-centennial. The poster said there would be an open-air concert featuring the rock-group "SAVAGE" under the stars at 9:00 P.M. at a park on the banks of the Mississippi.

Cindy and I were having such a wonderful time together, we quickly decided to stay for the concert. We killed a few hours by driving over to the Illinois side of the Mississippi River, bought a few bottles of wine to enjoy during the concert, then drove to a beautiful beach area where we could hear the concert just on the other side of the river.

There were a hundred or so other people who had gathered in the area to hear the music as well. We found the perfect spot, built a fire, drank our wine, hand-fed each other some grapes, talked, joked, laughed, and were having as wonderful a time as either of us could ever imagine.

We went swimming in the Mississippi, then held each other close as we dried out by the fire. When the concert was ready to get underway, we sat on the beach, leaning our backs against an old log, had some more wine, and enjoyed the music flowing from the other side of the river.

When the concert was over, there were fireworks celebrating the bi-centennial. Cindy and I had no idea that the fireworks display was planned, and it was a surprise that we both sat back and delighted in watching.

Once the fireworks were over, a Park Ranger came by to make everyone leave the park for the evening. Cindy told the Ranger she was a police officer, showed him her I.D. and the Ranger said we could stay for another hour.

Everyone had to clear the beach area and park, so Cindy and I were the only two left. We sat by the fire, held each other in our arms, kissed passionately time and again for the entire hour, and the time escaped. What was an hour seemed to be only minutes, and the Ranger returned to say we would have to leave.

We thanked him for allowing us to stay the extra time, then drove back to the Missiouri side of the river. We drove to a place high upon a ridge with a bluff overlooking the Mississippi called "Lover's Leap." We got there close to midnight, and there were only three other couples there to share the marvelous view.

162

It was a star-filled sky above us on that clear and warm night. We watched the tugs and barges work their way down the Mississippi, headed to Memphis, New Orleans, the Gulf of Mexico and destinations beyond. We watched the falling stars descend from the heavens, and the glow of the moon as it cascaded down the Mississippi with it's reflection. All these-simple things, but so romantic when shared with someone who makes you feel the way Cindy made me feel in that early morning hour.

We stayed on that bluff until around three A.M. holding each other and kissing. We headed back home, and for what seemed to be the longest time, the drive was silent. I knew what I was thinking, and something inside me said Cindy was thinking the same things as I was. I was thinking of how great our day together had been, how romantic everything seemed to be when the two of us shared them, and how I couldn't imagine a more romantic moment than the one we were now sharing. How romantic it was driving in total silence, with, other than those romantic thoughts of Cindy, only the whine of the tires on the pavement making any impression on my mind.

As I said, some how I just knew she was having the same thoughts as I, and I enjoyed knowing that. I turned on the radio and tuned in a soft rock station as Cindy lay her head on my shoulder. We drove on a little farther, then I pulled into a roadside picnic area. We sat on the picnic table and talked very little before we began holding and kissing each other once again.

We were both exhausted from the long day and drove to a nearby motel where we spent what was left of the early morning. When we awoke, we drove on to St. Louis, stopped for a late breakfast, then I took her home.

That was in 1984, and to this day, I have never experienced anything more romantic than that short trip to Hannibal, Missouri. I now live in Tennessee, Cindy still lives in Missouri, and we only see each other occasionally. Though we don't get to see each other often, I think of her frequently, and we have remained the best of friends.

I have come to realize that romance is in the eye of the beholder. And what is romantic to one may not be to another. But no matter the occasion, or the timing of it, if you're with someone that you truly enjoy being with—someone who makes you feel good just being around them-they will put you in a romantic mood.

That being the case, any trip, no matter how short or long the trip may be, can be romantic.

As a matter of fact, any time the two of you are together can be and should be a romantic moment. It doesn't have to be a trip. Romantic moments can happen anywhere, any-time. All it takes to set the mood is to share the moment with someone who puts you in it!

A Note to the Readers

It has been a real pleasure to share my romantic ideas with you. As I said before, I received my ideas about romance in various ways. Some were passed on to me by my friends, some were sent to me by people I didn't even know when they heard I was writing this book, but most of them were dreamed up my me in my own romantic mind.

I was surprised at how quickly the word got out that I was writing a book on romantic ideas and notions, and how so many people wanted to contact me and pass on their own ideas.

If you are one of the people who has his/her own notions about how to be romantic and please your lover, and want to share them with me, do so by writing to the address listed below. I'd love to hear from you!

Thanks,
Barry Rosen
(THE KING OF ROMANCE)

THE KING OF ROMANCE

WRITE TO: BARRY ROSEN
CENTURY VILLAGE EAST
NEWPORT Q. SUITE 1077
DEERFIELD BEACH, FL 33442

The King of Romance Fan Club

Dear Fan:

Here it is!!! The King of Romance Fan Club Entry Form. Please complete the bottom section and return to the address below, so that your lifetime membership card, autographed photo, t-shirt, biography, newletters, and 100 Rolls of Kodak Film will be shipped to you as soon as possible (see last page for more details). Along with your entry form, please enclose your one time membership fee of $25.00 in the form of a check or money order. Please allow 6-8 weeks for delivery. The King of Romance thanks you for your support.

Kindest Regards,

Barry Rosen
The King of Romance

Send to: **The King of Romance, Centursy Village East, Newport Q Suite 1077, Deerfield Beach, FL 33442**; Plus $3.50 for Shipping & Handling, allow 6-8 Weeks for Delivery.

Name_____

Address_____

City _____ State _____ Zip _____

Telephone ( )_____

Male_____ Female_____ Birthdate_____

Extra Large T-shirt Available **Only.**

Help us know who is Romantic...

Name_____

Address_____

City_____State_____ Zip_____

Age (Circle one)

18 under   19-21   22-27   28-35   36-42   43-50   50-over

Single _____   Married _____ Do You Have Kids?____
HowLong?_____

Sex   ❑Male   ❑Female

How did you hear about the book?

❑ TV   ❑ Radio   ❑Newspaper   ❑Magazines
❑ Friend   ❑ Flyer   ❑Poster
❑ Other_____

What TV shows do you watch?
❑ Soaps ❑ Daytime Talk Shows ❑Late Night Talk Shows
❑ News ❑ MTV ❑ Other _____

Fill this out and send to the King of Romance, Century Village, Newport Q Suite 1077, Deerfield Beach, FL 33442 and you will get 10 Rolls of Kodak film (see last page for more details)

Add $2.00 for shipping and handling, allow 6-8 weeks for delivery.

Order a book directly from the King of Romance for Birthday, Anniversary, or for Holiday presents:

❏ 1 book for $9.95 plus shipping and handling
❏ 2 to 4 books for $8.95 each plus shipping and handling
❏ 5 to 24 books for $6.00 each plus shipping and handling
❏ 25 to 49 books for $5.75 each plus shipping and handling
shipping and handling is $2.00 per book.

Send to:
The King of Romance
Century Village East
Newport Q Suite 1077
Deerfield Beach, Florida 33442

And We'll Give You Our Film Free

The King of Romance offer can be yours just for participating in this important processing survey.

The King of Romance gives you the latest high-tech Kodak Color Watch Developing on all your processing needs. A free roll, and up to 40% off Kodak's list for every roll sent in for developing, (Limit 100) With free mailer envelopes. Plus 20 beautiful enlargements and 3 photo puzzles of your favorite photo's absolutely free.

So hurry take advantage of this special offer today. Because everybody can use a little film.